C000185560

Hampshire Villages

A Portrait

Hampshire Villages

Villages

A Portrait

MIKE HOPE

Breedon Books
Publishing Company
Derby

First published in Great Britain by
The Breedon Books Publishing Company Limited
44 Friar Gate, Derby, DE1 1DA.
1995

© Mike Hope, 1995

All Rights Reserved. No part of this publication may be reproduced,
stored in a retrieval system, or transmitted in any form, or by any
means, electronic, mechanical, photocopying, recording or otherwise
without the prior permission in writing of the Copyright holders,
nor be otherwise circulated in any form or binding or cover other
than in which it is published and without a similar condition being
imposed on the subsequent publisher.

ISBN 1 85983 019 6

Printed and bound in Great Britain by
Butler & Tanner Ltd, Frome and London
Cover printed by Premier Print, Nottingham.

Contents

Dedication

To my parents for their constant support and initially instilling a deep love of my native county

Acknowledgements

My deep gratitude for the help given in various ways, is extended to the following:-

Chris Mills, Dave Savidge and Rob Newton, for the developing of the films and the printing of endless contact strips and photographs. Mike Woodhead for rescuing the text after I had caused total chaos, on more than one occasion with the 'pageflow' on the computer and his transferring of files from one format to another. Rob Newton once again for many hours spent in digitising all the maps. The Nottingham Trent University, for its support.

My father for not only accompanying me on a number of field trips but also for the lengthy task of proofing my manuscript. John Heath the series editor for his approaching me to undertake the project in the first place and his necessary constant exhortations.

Finally my entire long suffering family – my parents, my father-in-law, my wife and my two young sons, who have often accompanied me on trips, put up with return visits, to get that all important photo and my constant anti-social vigil hunched over the lap top computer.

Mike Hope. February 1995

Introduction

During the final stages of the research and writing of this book, Hampshire and in particular one of its villages, Southwick, held centre stage for much of the world during the run up to the fiftieth anniversary celebrations for the D-Day commemorations. A few weeks later, Hampshire was again for a day, the centre of international attention as it hosted a stage of the Tour De France, and a whole string of villages and scenically stunning countryside were shown to the world at large.

Hampshire has for long periods been centre stage in terms of British and indeed international history. Winchester was for sometime capital in its own right and then joint capital with London.

The county has produced or been home to a disproportionate number of famous men and women. It is the home of the Royal Navy and the Army. As a result virtually no village in Hampshire is without some famous connection.

Outside of agriculture, and to a lesser degree fishing, shipbuilding and brewing, the county has no large, traditional industries, no mineral deposits. Its forests have from the earliest been utilised for shipbuilding, which caused one of Hampshire's set piece villages, Bucklers Hard to be laid out. The twentieth century with its electronics industries, IBM, Plessey, GEC, Ferranti's etc have tended to congregate in the south-eastern indust-rialised part or around the new town development at Basingstoke. What this means is that surprisingly large tracts of Hampshire are relatively unspoilt. Areas such as the New Forest and the Chalk Downlands of much of central and north-western Hampshire are virtually unspoilt. The combination of these large areas of unspoilt predominantly agri-cultural landscape, coupled with the geological diversity of the county, means that there are a wealth of text book examples of villages.

The first thing to say about this book is that it is not just another book on Hampshire Villages. There are to my knowledge at least half a dozen books on the subject readily available. Jo Draper's *Hampshire the Complete Guide* springs most readily to mind. Nor is this another book which deals with the unusual and secret Hampshire as these too have already been done to death. What I have set out to do is to is make a choice of not just the most scenically stunning villages, but those which exemplify the geology and makeup of the surrounding countryside. Those which have seen major events in history. Those which possess out-standing examples of particular architectural styles. Those who claim the birth and final resting places of key figures. To this list of pre-requisites can be added a number of villages whose claim can be just one of ordinariness, a

Hampshire ordinariness. In short, this book sets out to whet the appetite, through words and pictures of the abundance of riches which has been bestowed upon Hampshire. The process of selection of around sixty villages has been both tortuous and slow. One of the first things I had to do was unfortunately remove from the list, those bewitching small market towns of which Hampshire is so well stocked; New Alresford, Bishops Waltham, Whitchurch, Odiham, Stockbridge, Petersfield, Romsey, Ringwood, Emsworth and Lyndhurst to name but a few. I have tried to keep personal preference and bias to a minimum and hopefully have succeeded in presenting a selection of villages which provide a balanced cross-section of Hampshire's riches.

Of the villages I have chosen the majority nestle in the valleys of some of the most famous fishing rivers in the world, the Avon, Itchen, Test, as well as the less well known Meon Valley. For me the Meon Valley is perhaps the prettiest part of Hampshire.

That I have only included six villages on Hampshire's seaboard is indicative of the fact that nearly all of Hampshire's urban development straddles its coastline. Between them Portsmouth, Southampton and Bournemouth's increasing suburban tentacles have mercilessly devoured the countryside and seaboard between them. The coastline, with the exception of the western stretch of Hampshire, where the cliffs rise at Milford on Sea and Barton on Sea, is geologically speaking a coastline of deep river estuaries and by the time it reaches its eastern end a coastline of secretive inlets, mud fringed creeks and very large harbours.

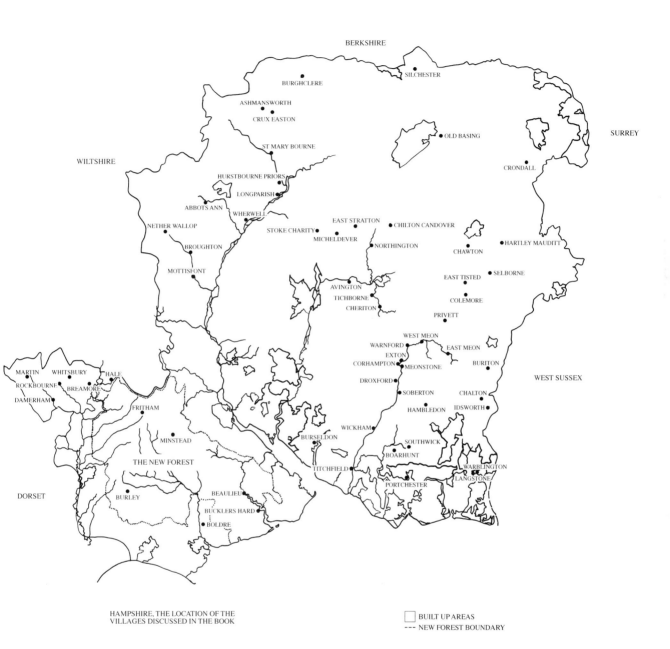

BERKSHIRE

SILCHESTER

BURGHCLERE

ASHMANSWORTH

CRUX EASTON

OLD BASING

WILTSHIRE

ST MARY BOURNE

CRONDALL

HURSTBOURNE PRIORS

LONGPARISH

ABBOTS ANN

WHERWELL

EAST STRATTON

CHILTON CANDOVER

STOKE CHARITY

NETHER WALLOP

MICHELDEVER

NORTHINGTON

HARTLEY MAUDITT

BROUGHTON

CHAWTON

MOTTISFONT

EAST TISTED

SELBORNE

AVINGTON

TICHBORNE

COLEMORE

CHERITON

PRIVETT

WEST MEON

WARNFORD

EAST MEON

EXTON

CORHAMPTON

MEONSTONE

BURITON

MARTIN

WHITSBURY

HALE

DROXFORD

ROCKBOURNE

BREAMORE

DAMERHAM

FRITHAM

SOBERTON

CHALTON

HAMBLEDON

IDSWORTH

WICKHAM

MINSTEAD

BURSELDON

SOUTHWICK

THE NEW FOREST

BOARHUNT

DORSET

TITCHFIELD

WARBLINGTON

LANGSTONE

PORTCHESTER

BURLEY

BEAULIEU

BUCKLERS HARD

BOLDRE

HAMPSHIRE, THE LOCATION OF THE
VILLAGES DISCUSSED IN THE BOOK

SURREY

WEST SUSSEX

☐ BUILT UP AREAS
--- NEW FOREST BOUNDARY

The Avon Valley and its tributaries

The River Avon, which has its origins in the chalk valleys of Wiltshire, with the exception of Fordingbridge and Ringwood has, during its Hampshire sojourn, no large settlements on its banks. On the western bank a singularly large tongue of land stabs into the neighbouring counties of Dorset and Wiltshire. The parishes of Martin and Damerham were transferred to Hampshire at the whim of some county planner in 1895. Hampshire suffered at the hands of the planners in 1974 with the loss of Bournemouth and Christchurch to Dorset. This tongue of land to the west of the Avon valley, consists of some outstanding chalk valleys, whose streams swell the Avon below Fordingbridge. Damerham, Martin, Whitsbury and Rockbourne reside in this area and are all represented. In addition Breamore and Hale, which sit virtually opposite one another are for reasons of geology and topography very different. Hale sits on the eastern scarp of the river valley, part of the New Forest visually and geologically, if not administratively. Breamore on the other hand sits in the Avon Valley amongst the lush watermeadows and rising up the slopes towards the house.

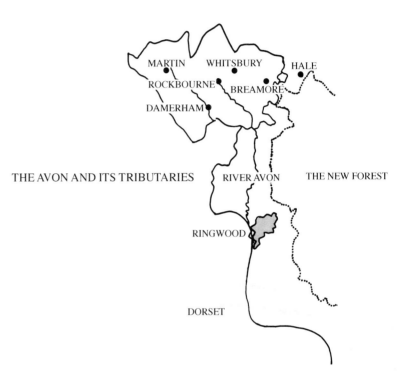

THE AVON AND ITS TRIBUTARIES

Behind this the hills, now chalk, rise to Breamore Down, with its Miz-Maze and Iron Age Camp. Beyond this the chalk downland with steep-sided valleys enclosing Whitsbury and Rockbourne, opens out to the north-west and Martin. To the south-west Damerham sits amongst the lush watermeadows of the River Allen. From the road from Whitsbury to Rockbourne, distant views westward, encompas the rolling chalk downlands of the Cranborne Chase and South Wiltshire. Martin really is the final settlement in western Hampshire, far closer to Salisbury and Shaftsbury, than Winchester or Southampton.

Breamore – View of the old railway station, thirty years after closure.

Breamore

Breamore lies largely amongst the meadows of the River Avon and up the western chalk slopes of the valley, it is one of the most impressive and historic of all Hampshire's villages. There is evidence for at least three thousand years of continuous occupation in the parish. It is not a nucleated settlement but rather spreads out around a number of features. The more modern part of the village lines the busy A338 Salisbury to Ringwood road. As a result Breamore's points of interest are spread out over a relatively wide area.

Starting with the most prominent feature of the village, Breamore House. It sits above the village in an elevated position. It is built of warm pale red brick with stone dressings, a textbook example of an Elizabethan 'E' shaped manor house of some size. It was built between 1580 and 1583 for William Doddington, who was Auditor of the Tower Mint. Although there was a serious fire in 1856, the house was sympathetically restored. Internally the house, which is open during the summer months each year, possesses a wealth of interesting features and objects collected by the Hulse family during their

Breamore – The mill on the River Avon.

nine generations of occupancy. To my mind it is unfortunate that you are given a guided tour which can be excruciating. At the back of the house is a very prominent Victorian brick three-storey octagonal clock tower. The top is surmounted by a white wooden cupola. Adjacent to this is the Georgian stable block. Within this is contained a large exhibition of carriages, the most spectacular exhibit being the Red Rover stagecoach which ran between London and Southampton in the early years of the nineteenth century.

To the south-east of the house is the more recent development of The Countryside Museum. Set up in some of the former walled gardens it is an outstanding display, not only of large scale artifacts such as tractors and steam traction but also the re-creation of a village street and various workshops, such as a blacksmith and wheelwright's. This museum should not be missed and becomes even more spectacular on special event days such as a vintage steam rally.

Just to the east of the museum and nestling in the trees by the gate to the house, lies St Mary's Church. This is the single most important Saxon church in Hampshire. It was previously dedicated to St Mary and St Michael. It dates from the very late tenth or early eleventh century. Its construction is largely of flint infill with a number of reused Roman bricks and tiles. The church was until the fifteenth century somewhat larger, it was then that

Breamore – Cottages in Upper Street.

the northern porticus which served as a transept was demolished along with a baptistry which stood at the west end of the nave. The south porch was added sometime in the twelfth century and converted into a two-storey building probably in the fifteenth century. These alterations and the restoration of 1897, have left much of the Saxon fabric visible. The south transept or porticus has good long and short work (these are large stone quoins laid vertically and horizontally at the corners of buildings) and a good small double splayed Saxon window. There are a number of other double splayed windows, long and short work and pilasters visible in the external fabric.

Internally it is the south transept arch which is the most striking pre-conquest feature. The capitals of the arch are made from two very large stones. It is on this arch that the famous inscription can be seen. 'Her Swutelath Seo Gecwydraednes The'. Translated this reads, Here is made plain the Covenant to thee. This inscription has been dated by the style of the lettering to the latter stages of the reign of Ethelred II (979-1016). The porch was originally built in the early twelfth century with the Norman doorway bearing witness to this. In the fifteenth century an upper level and floor were added. This was to protect and at the same time venerate the large and impressive pre-conquest carved rood figures. These figures would have originally depicted the

Virgin Mary and St John either side of the Crucified Christ. Above the figure of Christ was the Manus Dei (the Hand of God). The figures were unfortunately carefully hacked off during the reformation so that now there is just the outline. These figures on this scale are a Hampshire speciality, (the other three surviving in a likewise mutilated form can be seen at Romsey Abbey, Headbourne Worthy and Winchester Cathedral). They are unique in Europe, let alone Britain at this point in the eleventh century. All round the figures at Breamore are the remains of later wall paintings, depicting countryside, buildings and a church. There are a number of other interesting features which make this church a must for any visitor.

The long line of cottages running south from the museum in what is known as Upper Street, are largely seventeenth century in date and nearly all are thatched. These still belong to the Breamore estate. South-east of the estate towards the road is a large stretch of open ground containing a number of ponds and the village cricket ground. This is known as the Marsh. Cricket has been played here since the 1830s. The village pub on the main road is aptly named the Bat and Ball. It is a Victorian mock Tudor style building. Its pub sign is a copy of the famous Boy with the Bat painting which can be seen in Breamore House. The painting along with another early eighteenth century one owned by the MCC is considered the earliest cricketing painting in existence. Opposite the pub are the village stocks. To the east of the main road amongst the water meadows of the Avon, sits the seemingly well-preserved derelict railway station, looking much like it did in 1963 when the line was axed. Nearby is a large and impressive water mill complex which can be seen from the road.

Nothing now remains of the Augustinian priory which existed in the village from 1130 to 1536. The site near the river was partially excavated in 1898. One further site of great interest in the village, is the justly famous Miz-Maze high up on the down behind Breamore House. Its origins are at least mediæval. Quite what its use was remains the subject of much speculation, but once their existence was commonplace across England. It consists of eleven concentric rings leading to a central mound.

All of Breamore is justifiably now protected as a conservation area and any exploration of the village is well repaid.

Damerham

Set amongst the floodplain and therefore the meadows of the infant River Allan, the village clusters around its pub, bridges and village school. Away to the east on higher ground is set the church and behind it, on higher ground still, is a large house, which can be seen clearly from the road, revealing mediæval stonework of the highest craftsmanship. These Decorated period

Damerham – Parish church of St George from across the watermeadows.

arches are a direct link with Glastonbury Abbey, as during the mediæval period the manor was held by the Abbots of Glastonbury.

The church of St George reveals architecture from many periods. Its fine Perpendicular period east end, Perpendicular porch and west window. The large squat Norman tower because of later additions, now appears dwarfed. Inside the porch above the door is set a Norman tympanum depicting a Crusader slaying a Saracen. The roofs are good examples of wagon roofs.

Hale

On the eastern scarp of the Avon Valley and on the edge of the New Forest, the village lies largely around a large irregular green. The setting of thatched cottages, sheep, cattle and above all New Forest ponies grazing the green is idyllic and would merit inclusion for its aesthetic charms alone. But Hale has two further splendid treasures tucked away right on the edge of the Avon Valley scarp. As you drive down the the side of the valley, you pass a gate lodge with an overgrown drive and further on as the road twists down, you come to another lodge at the start of

Hale – Hale House entrance front.

an impressive drive of trees. At the bottom of these is the splendidly situated Hale Park. It was the home of Thomas Archer, who was in the early eighteenth century, arguably the most influential architect in Britain.

The classical Georgian house one sees, is however largely a later remodelling by Henry Holland. The house consists of a central block with a large three bay portico with four columns rising through two storeys. Either side of the central block are lower (one and a half storey) blocks with three bay pediments. The courtyard thus created is enclosed by a low stone balustrade which creates a wonderful Georgian ensemble. Although today strictly private, it was briefly at the

end of the 1960s open on a regular basis. I well remember the elegance of the staircase hall and the view from the windows of the canted bay in the drawing room across the Avon Valley. Lower down the hill and to one side of the house, sits the cruciform church. That it is more of a Greek temple, is due to Thomas Archer, who built it in 1717. St Mary's Church is not quite as Archer left it. The Victorians altered a number of the windows and filled some of them with stained glass. As to monuments there are many but those in the south transept are especially worth looking at. Set against the south wall is the monument to Thomas Archer. It dates from 1739 and consists of a background grey obelisk, with a reclining male figure

Hale – View across the village green.

dressed in Roman apparel. Either side are two female figures which represent his two wives.

Nearby is the monument to Henry Archer, who died in 1768. This consists of a female figure standing next to an urn. Finally the memorial to Joseph May, who died in 1796. This is of exquisite design (by James Wyatt and carved by Sir Richard Westmacott) Simply an urn on a base which has a rams head at each corner. Neo-Classicism at its chaste best. The churchyard falls away steeply, and through the trees, glimpses of the Avon on its serpentine route can be caught, as well as the western side of the valley and the Breamore estate, a truly sublime final resting place.

Martin

In terms of geography this is Hampshire's final western fling – a tongue of land which until 1895 was a part of Wiltshire. It is bordered on two sides by Wiltshire and by Dorset on another. Under ten miles from Salisbury and only some fifteen from Shaftesbury, it feels more like a village in western Wiltshire than one in Hampshire.

Martin – The village green.

It is set around a village green and most of the houses have lawned banks. The village has no pub but a large club on the western edge. Its houses reveal a varied range of vernacular styles. Many of the buildings possess stone mullions and transoms and it is this feature which gives it the feel of a west Wiltshire village. Scattered amongst the village are larger, more architecturally impressive houses.

The church of All Saints is set back some distance from the village green, but has a strong visual impact, with its mediæval west tower and tall stone spire, itself unusual for a Hampshire village. The tower is in the lower stages thirteenth century, with the upper stage being Perpendicular. There was a spire in the fifteenth century, but this was replaced by the present larger octagonal spire in 1787. The chancel was extended in both the thirteenth and fourteenth centuries. The south transept and porch were added in the fourteenth century and the large north aisle added in the sixteenth century. The church was repeatedly restored during the second half of the nineteenth century.

Near the west tower lies the grave of William Lawes. His son James was the real life inspiration for 'Isaac Balcombe', who was the central figure in W.H.Hudson's *A Shepherd's Life*.

Rockbourne – The hillside setting of St Andrew's Church and churchyard.

Rockbourne

Set in its deep downland valley, Rockbourne must rank as one of the set pieces of Hampshire. A classic linear village, it lines the valley bottom either side of its river. A string of largely thatched, brick cottages create endless photographic opportunities. Dotted amongst these, are larger more substantial eighteenth and nineteenth-century houses. At the southern end of the village are the remains of Rockbourne Roman Villa with its small museum, administered by Hampshire County Council. When I was first taken there as a small boy, the site was privately owned and fully uncovered. Roman coins from the large

hoard discovered in an earthenware jar, on site, were on sale to help the cost of excavations. I still possess my Tetricus II bought for 17s 6d. The site, largely filled in today, is I think rather sanitised and has lost much of the excitement of twenty-five years ago. Nearby are the forlorn gate lodges to West Park, once the home of the Eyre-Coote family. The house having been requisitioned during the war was demolished in 1945. In the park and visible for many miles is the recently restored pillar set up as a memorial to General Sir Eyre Coote in 1827.

At the opposite end of the village, high on the eastern hillside is the church of St

Rockbourne – Village cottages with stream in foreground.

Rockbourne – The forlorn gate lodges to the long demolished West Park.

Andrew. The churchyard slopes steeply around the church and from the top of the churchyard are extensive views across the village and valley. The church dates from the Saxon period, and there is externally the blocked arched head of a former doorway, set above a thirteenth-century door in the north wall. Internally the arch into the north transept is also Saxon. The church at this period would have been cruciform. It was largely rebuilt and enlarged in the twelfth century, with the south aisle being added in the thirteenth century. The bell turret which is wooden, dates from 1613. The whole church was sensitively restored by C.E.Ponting

Whitsbury

The road from Rock-bourne climbs steadily up the side of a chalk ridge. There follows an invigorating ride along the top of the ridge with expansive views in most directions. Passing a neatly laid out group of farmworkers' cottages and adjoining farm, you rise further through trees before a steep plunge

in 1893. Internally the church contains a number of interesting features which include a good Flemish triptych dating from the early sixteenth century.

Near to the church, the Manor House, forms a very interesting group of buildings which exhibit many periods dating from the mediæval period, including a chapel and some fourteenth-century barns. The central portion of the house is Elizabethan.

Whitsbury – St Leonard's Church 1878. The brick west tower has very unusual chamfered corners.

Whitsbury – View of the Old Rectory, from the path to St Leonard's Church.

down the valley and thus to Whitsbury. As a village it is dominated by horses; studs and stables abound. Driving through the village apart from being struck by the number of stables you would not feel that the village was in any way out of the ordinary. However take the public footpath up the steep eastern slope and you pass an impressive late eighteenth/early nineteenth-century mansion, set in landscaped grounds.

The footpath becomes steeper as the top of the ridge is gained and before you is a totally rebuilt largely nondescript Victorian church of St Leonard. It was completely rebuilt in 1878 and virtually no old features were retained or re-used. The brick tower is of note in that it has chamfered corners, on the upper stage. The views from the churchyard across the roof of the New Forest to the distant Isle of Wight are sublime. Closer to in the prospect the surrounding paddocks are full of horses.

Whitsbury – Detail of gravestone fragment propped against the church tower.

The New Forest

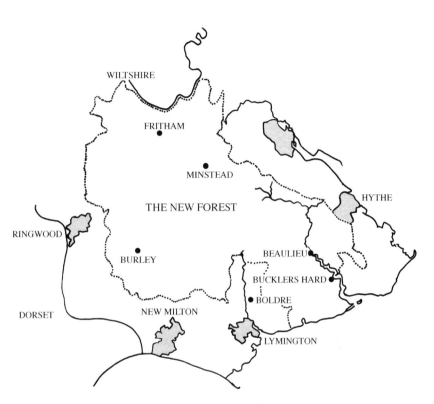

For nine hundred years and more of the New Forest's existence, it has been administered and guarded by the Verderers Court. It has from its beginnings as a Royal hunting preserve been protected and therefore spared both agricultural and urban development. It is today some one hundred and fifty square miles, designated as an area of outstanding natural beauty. The present boundaries contain five of the six villages discussed in this section, the sixth, Boldre, sits in identical countryside and possesses all the same features, but falls outside the designated boundaries. There are only two large settlements in the Forest, Lyndhurst, which acts as a sort of capital, with its Verderers Court, magnificent church, museum, shops and hotels, and Brockenhurst which has expanded rapidly and also possesses a railway station.

The Forest itself is surrounded by large urban areas, Southampton and Totton to the north, Hythe and the industrial complexes of Fawley and Calshot to the east. To the south is the delightful town of Lymington and to complete the picture, to the west, New Milton and Ringwood.

Geologically, it is a large area of Tertiary sands and gravels, which have given rise to classic heathland scenery. These heathlands are at their highest, wild and remote in the north-western area, around Fritham, Bramshaw, and Godshill. The expansive views reveal an undulating countryside, with in all directions, dense plantations of largely conifers. To the south and east the Forest has become more subdued with deciduous and mixed plantations, along side natural woodlands. These are interspersed with heathland and wide open stretches of turf. On the coastal fringe, the Forest is indented by the Beaulieu and Lymington rivers.

The forest, which was enclosed by

Beaulieu – The former outer gatehouse, with a nineteenth-century clock turret.

William the Conqueror, is today, a combination of heathland, woods, of both natural and Forestry Commission variety, large areas of turf and a fairly varied topography.

The six villages selected, range from the justly famous Beaulieu and Bucklers Hard in the southern area of the Forest, to Fritham and Minstead, in the north-western area. Burley has for most of this century, like Beaulieu and Bucklers Hard, relied on the tourist trade, whilst Boldre has developed to encompass a number of hamlets, yet remaining scattered throughout a combination of both agricultural and wooded, rural scenery.

Beaulieu – View through the Chapter House arches to the cloister and the former refectory, now the parish church of the Blessed Virgin and Child.

Beaulieu

Arguably the tourist attraction of the New Forest area, it is really a series of interlocking elements. There is the village, which grew up first around the great monastic foundation, and most recently became a nineteenth-century estate village serving, Palace House, the home of the Lords Montagu. This, in the last forty years, has grown to become one of the great tourist destinations of Britain, being

Beaulieu – Palace House.

the home of The National Motor Museum. The Abbey ruins, which were after all, the reason for the development of the site, are now an interesting attraction in their own right, with the cloisters, lay brothers quarters, which house a splendid exhibition, and the former refectory, which serves as the parish church.

Starting with the monastic ruins. The abbey was founded in 1204, by King John for the Cistercian order. It quickly, with such august royal patronage, developed on a very large scale. The church was some three hundred and thirty-six feet long with an apsed ambulatory and radiating chapels in the latest French fashion. Of this very little survives apart from the ground plan and low walls, as the site was

extensively plundered for its stone in the building of Hurst and Calshot castles. The cloister is much better preserved, with the triple arches of the chapter house entrance being particularly beautiful. The lay brothers' quarters is still, for a good portion of its length, standing to full height and roofed. This contains the exhibition on the ground floor and on the upper floor, the tie-beamed roof looks down on what is now a restaurant. In the south range, the day stairs start their forlorn climb to nowhere. Next to this is the perfectly preserved Monks' refectory which is now the parish church for Beaulieu. Dedicated to the Blessed Virgin and Child. It is a particularly striking piece of Early English architecture, dating from

Beaulieu – The main village street, with the Palace House roofscape beyond.

c.1230. The church is a single room, some one hundred and twenty-five feet long, and is lit by tall single lancets. Built into the thickness of the west wall is a series of arches carried on Purbeck marble shafts, which light the stairs to a pulpit, from which originally, lessons would have been read to the monks eating below. The roof is fourteenth century.

The Palace House, was originally the great gatehouse for the monastery. Massively extended in the late nineteenth century in a Scottish Baronial style complete with towers, conical roofs and mullioned windows, the scene is completed by the pond, which is formed by the damming of the river, which is up to this point a navigable tidal estuary. There is a picturesque outer gatehouse, restored and given a clock tower in the nineteenth

century. The interior of Palace House, is full of interesting furniture, pictures, etc collected by the Montagu family over the last four hundred years.

The present Lord Montagu developed his passion for motor transport into the now world famous National Motor Museum. This is now housed in a purpose-built modern building some distance to the north of the Abbey and house. In addition to the dazzling array of vehicles, there is a monster model railway display in a separate building, along with a host of other activities. All of these are connected by a monorail and there are splendid modern visitor facilities to round off the site.

The village sits across the pond from the Palace House, which forms an extremely picturesque backdrop. The village is built largely of brick, with the Montagu Arms Hotel, situated on the bend into the village. The main street is made up of typical late Victorian estate cottages. Returning to the dam, the views down the tidal estuary to the mature woods, with moored boats is particularly beautiful. This beauty continues on down to Bucklers Hard and beyond, with the estuary and much of the adjoining land being in the ownership of Lord Montagu.

Boldre

Although situated in the New Forest it actually falls outside of the officially designated Forest boundary. The countryside, especially around the church in the north of the parish, is typical of the Forest, gently undulating countryside, a mixture of open heaths, dense mixed woods, streams and agricultural land. The parish is virtually bisected by the Lymington River. It is very spread out neither nucleated or linear. It is in fact made up of a group of hamlets, including Pilley, Portmore, Bull Hill, Bailey, Walhampton, Sandy Down and Boldre itself. The housing is, as can be imagined, widely spread with many large houses. Pilley is the most village like part of the parish, with a pub and rows of cottages. This part of Boldre is also home to Spinners, which is a well-known wood-land garden, open to the public on a regular basis.

It is however, the church in the north-eastern corner of the parish which is Boldre's chief feature of interest. The church dates from the Norman period, although most of the fabric dates from the thirteenth century. The chancel which was rebuilt on a larger scale in the fourteenth century was totally rebuilt in 1855. The lower stage of the tower dates from the fourteenth century with the upper stage which is built of brick dating from 1697.

Internally, the roofs are of note, being wagon roofs which date from the fourteenth century. Displayed in the south aisle there is a Breeches Bible dated 1596.

The church serves as the only place with a memorial to the officers and men who died on board *HMS Hood* when she was sunk in action against the German battleship *Bismarck* on 24 May 1941. The reason for Boldre being home to the memorial is that for many years prior to the war Vice-admiral L.E.Holland CB and his family were regular worshippers at the church. Besides the painting, photographs, and two vice-Admiral's lanterns, there is an *Illuminated Book of Remembrance* which lists the names of all 1,416 officers and men on board the *Hood*. An annual service of remembrance takes place on or near the anniversary of the sinking.

Boldre's chief claim to fame however, lies in its rector in the last quarter of the eighteenth century. the Reverend William Gilpin. He was rector here between 1777 to 1804. He was famous as an artist, writer and one of the prime movers in the development of the Picturesque Movement. His tomb lies on the north side of the churchyard.

Buckler's Hard

The seaboard village *par excellence* of Hampshire and a fascinating example of a planned eighteenth-century industrial complex. Part of the Beaulieu estates owned by Lord Montagu, it was one of his ancestors, the second Duke of Montagu, who brought the village into being. He was the owner of great estates in the West Indies including the islands of St Vincent and St Lucia. This coupled to the fact that his family inherited from the Abbots of Beaulieu the right to have a free harbour, and the fact that the neighbouring woods on his estates were full of prime oak trees, led the Duke to speculate in setting up what he hoped would develop into a fully-fledged free port and ship building facility to handle the produce from his vast West Indies estates.

The plan which had received a Royal Charter from George I was doomed with the invasion of those particular islands by the French. Although the port, which was to be named Montagu Town, never developed, due to the proximity of plentiful timber supplies, a good sheltered tidal estuary and the closeness of Portsmouth, the shipbuilding enterprise took off. To encourage people to move to what was after all a rather remote 'greenfield' site, the Duke offered inducements such as cheap rent and supplies of timber. The Wyatt family from nearby Southampton, were one of the first to move in in 1743. In 1745 the first naval ship *The Surprise* was launched. Although only of fourteen guns it marked the start of over a fifty-year relationship with the Admiralty. Bigger and bigger ships were built and launched including *The Agamemnon* (sixty-four guns) which was a true first-rate ship of the line. Indeed Bucklers Hard provided three ships that fought at Trafalgar, the previously mentioned *Agamemnon*, *Euryalas* and the *Swiftsure*.

It was however the Adams family, who moved to Bucklers Hard, that created its heyday. Henry Adams was responsible for the building of the aforementioned *Agamemnon* in 1781. All of this information and much more is superbly presented in the Maritime Museum, which is complete with models, diagrams, plans, books, tools etc. It is in fact the way in which you enter the sloping, wide street. Having worked your way through the museum, you enter a series of recreated eighteenth-century rooms, complete with realistic figures. The change from the almost claustrophobic and dim interiors to the wide grassy slope with the row of cottages on each side sloping down to the wide Beaulieu River, is stunning.

The village, if it can be called that, is no more than this wide expanse of sloping grass, lined by a row of Georgian red-brick cottages on either side. These cottages (one possesses the date 1774) are fairly uniform in appearance (although some have the addition of bay windows), white woodwork and the dormer windows punctuating the roofscape. Some of these houses still serve as private dwellings. Others have like the museum had their interiors restored to something like their eighteenth-century appearance, complete with furniture and artifacts. Halfway down on the left-hand side, one of the cottages hides behind its exterior, a bewitchingly beautiful chapel. The chapel previously served as the village dame's school, and before that in the heyday of the village, as a cobbler's shop. It was converted into a chapel in the late nineteenth century. The panelling behind the altar is late seventeenth century. Many objects and fittings have been offered as memorials to various people in the ensuing 100 years. One final note about the chapel is that under the floor lies, still to this day, a smugglers hole.

At the bottom of the left-hand block of cottages, is the former house of the master shipbuilder, Henry Adams. He built a banqueting house on to it, where he entertained two kings and a host of nobility. This survives today as a hotel. Below this are the remains of two of the slipways. Nearby a modern pontoon is the departure point for boat trips down the river towards the open sea. I cannot recommend too highly, the leisurely one hour round trip amongst the various yachts and pleasure boats moored in the river. It is also the only way to see the adjacent land and occasionally the large houses which are all private estates.

Burley

The picture postcard, tourist honeypot of the Forest, it has for most of this century relied on the passing tourist to bolster its rural activities. A confluence of roads and lanes set in classic undulating heaths and woods, it became in the 1950s famous for witchcraft. This was due to one woman, Sybil Leek, who, as a practising White Witch complete with a pet jackdaw, really put Burley on the map. Today, although over a decade since her death, and longer since she went to America, the village still boasts two shops with witchcraft connections, A Coven of Witches (which she named) and nearby Witchcraft. Neither shop seems to sell anything remotely connected with witches/ witchcraft being full of rather kitsch giftware and mementoes. Indeed, besides the numerous teashops there appear to be only shops selling the widest possible range of trinkets and gifts, from fudge to horsebrasses. All of which is more reminiscent of a seaside promenade.

The Queens Head pub is one of the Forest's most famous watering holes and has a long history of being a centre for smuggling activities. Across the valley from the village sits the nineteenth-century Burley Manor, now a hotel.

Burley – 'A Coven of Witches'.

Burley – 'Witchcraft' and its neighbouring shop.

It is however the countryside around Burley, especially that around the district known as Burley Street which holds the attention and brings me back repeatedly. Splendid stretches of lawn, streams and dense woods. To the west is Castle Hill which rises to just over three hundred feet and from its Iron Age rampart affords extensive views across the Forest.

Fritham

This is the less frequented north-western corner of the New Forest, the highlands of the Forest. A long, winding dead end lane, runs down past Fritham Lodge, a large and handsome turn of the century house, with a large and impressive water tower on one side (now a nursing home) and Fritham Farm on the other side which is a good Georgian building. The lane twists past farm buildings and views, across a combination of pastoral and forest landscape. Even in this remote spot is a bus stop, although on the numerous occasions I have traversed this lane I have

Fritham – The Royal Oak.

Fritham – Eyeworth Pond.

Fritham – A typical New Forest scene.

never seen a bus. As you reach the top of a small hill, there is a cluster of cottages and the village pub, The Royal Oak. Here the New Forest really reaches into the village. Stretches of turf are enclosed by dense patches of scrubby undergrowth and combinations of old oak and beech trees. Here and there are clumps of pine trees.

Livestock such as cows and enormous pigs, normally followed by numbers of piglets, forage about freely and mix with the many New Forest ponies which congregate around here. The road becomes smaller and less well made as you traverse the downward slope. To the left opens out classic New Forest heathland, boggy ground, heather, turf patches and clumps of trees, rising and falling away to the horizon and the large plantations. On the right-hand side the woodland comes right down to the road edge. At the bottom you are confronted by a very large pond which is man made. In fact it is not immediately recognisable, that the road, which travels on a short distance to the Edwardian cottages and finally Eyeworth Lodge, is carried on a fairly large dam. The reason for the existence of the pond and the houses was gunpowder. Between 1856 and 1923 this sylvan setting was the site for the production of smokeless gunpowder. Schulze's Gunpowder firm at one stage employed up to 100 people at this remote site. There were in the heyday of the factory over seventy buildings of which now there is almost no sign.

Today the pond is a haven for many types of bird and waterfowl. Take the path around the side of the lake, and cross very marshy ground, and you will find yourself in wonderfully remote woods where the chances of seeing another soul are rare. A circular walk which brings you in by the dam from the south-west, will lead you, if you are lucky, past one of the largest badger sets I have ever seen. From the mediæval period onwards, the waters of the stream which forms the lake, were considered to have curative properties. A chalybeate or holy well was established, and amongst other diseases the waters were supposed to have cured was leprosy. In the late nineteenth century it was thought to cure mange in dogs.

The brown water still runs plentifully today, any takers?

Minstead

A large straggling village scattered through this northern part of the New Forest, it is set in undulating countryside with the highest point crowned by the church and its surrounding large churchyard. The church of All Saints which undoubtedly served a very large part of the Forest, is for this village, large. It appears from the lychgate to be a very homely series of different sized gables, dormers and a large brick west tower. The tower itself has a date of 1774 and the nearby porch dates from 1683. If you continue to walk round the church via the east end you are confronted by a southward extension almost as long as the nave. This too dates from the 1790s. This aspect of the church also reveals the same homely aspect as the north side, complete with dormers and Georgian Gothick features.

Whilst in the churchyard a walk across to the large oak tree on the southern edge, brings you to a large cross. This marks the grave of Sir Arthur Conan Doyle, creator of Sherlock Holmes.

Returning to the church, the overwhelm-ing feeling of the interior is of the eighteenth century. It feels that in every conceivable

Minstead – The Trusty Servant pub sign.

place are pews and galleries, and to complete the picture a three-decker pulpit.

Immediately outside the churchyard, new housing in the guise of executive developments have started to infill. As you walk down the hill to the small green, on the left is the Trusty Servant pub. The building itself is of no real architectural pretension. However the pub sign is worthy of a second glance. The picture itself depicts a man in a doublet, with hooves for feet and a composite head, made up of a pig's head with rabbit's ears. Underneath the sign runs the following verse:-

> A trusty servants portrait would you see
> This emblamatic figure well survey
> The porkers snout not nice in diet shows
> The padlock shut no secret he'll disclose
> Patient the Ass his masters wrath will bear
> Swiftness in errand the staggs feet declare
> Loaded his left hand apt to labour saith
> The vest his neatness Open hand his faith

> Girt with his sword his shield upon his arm
> himself and master he'll protect from harm

On the outskirts of the village lies Furzey Gardens. It is famed for its heathers and azaleas but is worth a visit at any season. At the bottom of the undulating gardens, are a series of large children's houses and tree houses, big enough for almost any child of any age to squeeze into. A number of paths meander back up the site, past the large Edwardian house which now acts as a retreat centre. The original brick and timber cottage by the entrance, forms a museum, showing how primitive an existence was led in the past.

The large adjacent barn is now a Crafts centre, whose crafts range from the good to the banal.

One final point is that both the village and especially Furzey Gardens are blighted by the constant roar of the nearby trunk road/motorway.

The Test Valley and its tributaries

A river valley that is world famous to anglers, it curves round a great swathe of northern and western Hampshire, before reaching the sea at Southampton Water. For much of its length, it runs through classic chalk countryside and only possesses any degree of urban development at Romsey and again between Southampton and Totton, all at its southern end.

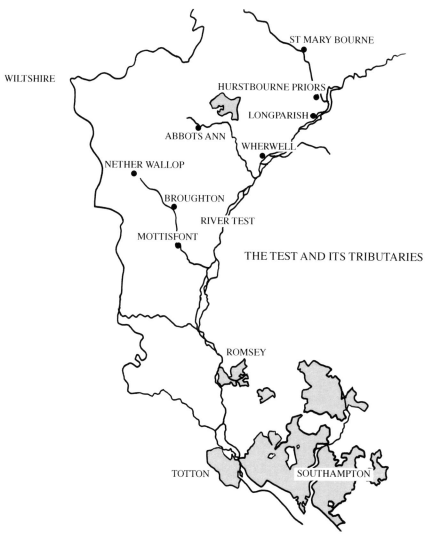

THE TEST AND ITS TRIBUTARIES

Besides spectacular countryside scenery, the river is liberally dotted with an endless succession of delightful villages. The various tributaries, the Wallop Brook and the Bourne Rivulet have the same features and cummulatively possess an almost embarrassing abundance of bewitchingly beautiful villages, with many interesting features. The final selection of just eight, Mottisfont, Broughton, Nether Wallop, Abbots Ann, Longparish, Wherwell, Hurstbourne Priors and St Mary Bourne, meant the exclusion of many others such as, Kings Somborne, Longstock, Middle and Over Wallop, Hurstbourne Tarrant and Freefolk, to mention but a few.

Abbots Ann – The Georgian (1716) west tower of St Mary's Church.

Abbots Ann

A large village which is predominantly half timber and thatch. The main street slopes down the hill toward the Pilhill Brook. The church of St Mary the Virgin is the main attraction. It is along with Avington Church, a text book example of Georgian architecture. It was entirely rebuilt in 1716 by Thomas Pitt, who had bought the estate with money he had amassed whilst Governor of Madras. He had made a vast sum by selling a very large diamond to the Regent of France. Apart from some pinnacles on the west tower, stained glass and additional tracery in the windows, the church amazingly escaped too much attention from the Victorians, to whom such a building was anathema.

The interior then still possesses the early Georgian feeling, lots of woodwork, box pews, and a west gallery supported on Tuscan columns. But for all this, Abbots Ann's claim to fame rests in the survival, a unique survival in Hampshire, and indeed a rare survival anywhere in England, of Virgin's Crowns or Maiden's Garlands. This once widespread tradition, was that when a man or woman, who had been born, baptised and died in the village and had remained unmarried, they were accorded the following rites. At their funeral procession, two young girls, dressed in white, carried the Virgin's Crown, suspended from a rod. It was made up of hazlewood and decorated with paper flowers. from this hung five parchment guantlets, which symbolised the act of challenging anyone who disputed the claim of a blemish free life. More of these crowns survive hanging from the nave roof than in any other church, the earliest dates from 1811 and the most recent 1973.

Broughton

This is the next village down stream from the Wallops. The valley is now very wide and shallow, the countryside lush. The village exhibits a nucleated settlement pattern unlike its neighbours, the Wallops. The way in which the church and churchyard sit amongst the houses of the main street is particularly delightful. Once again the overriding sense of architectural quality of the village is one of largely Georgian buildings with a good deal of Victorian and earlier cottages and houses.

The centre of the village has on one side the church and some Georgian cottages. On the other side of the road and set back some way is the Georgian Old Church farm, with a particularly fine door-hood. Nearby and on the corner is The Greyhound. Below the church a row of buildings and cottages gradually peters out and the Wallop Brook runs for a short while near to the road. North from the church there are a number of timber-framed cottages as well as some more

Broughton – Georgian cottages and the tower of St Mary's Church.

modern infill. The church is dedicated to St Mary. It dates from the twelfth century although the majority of the fabric dates from the thirteenth century. The west tower and the clerestory of the nave was added in the fifteenth century. Set into the tower, the earlier thirteenth century west door, with a good band of dog tooth pattern in one of the arch mouldings. The chancel was rebuilt in 1886. Internally the building is largely twelfth and thirteenth century, with, of especial note, a Dutch early sixteenth-century painting of *The Descent from the Cross*. This forms part of the reredos above the south aisle altar.

The churchyard possesses some good gravestones but the most important

Broughton – Thatched cob walling.

Broughton – The brick dovecote in the churchyard.

Broughton – View of the village and the Test Valley.

feature is north-east of the church. This is the dovecote. The present freestanding circular structure dates from 1684 when it replaced the dovecote which had in turn stood since 1340. The internal wooden rotating mechanism was restored in 1984. There are 482 nesting boxes built into the brickwork.

Hurstbourne Priors

Situated just above the point where the Bourne Rivulet makes its entry into the River Test, the setting is one of fairly lush meadows as the Bourne valley gives way to the Test valley. At the meeting point of two busy B class roads, the village hugs the B3048. Despite some recent infill, the village is largely the estate village which grew and flourished in the nineteenth century, outside the boundaries of Hurstbourne Park, which was the principal seat of the Earls of Portsmouth. The church sits against a backdrop of the heavily wooded slopes of the park, and is itself set down a drive of trees. Adjacent to the churchyard is the village cricket ground complete with a thatched pavilion.

The church has a large powerful Neo-Norman west tower dating from 1870. The west door is however, original. The chancel is thirteenth century and thus Early English in style, the north chapel

Hurstbourne Priors – View of the village from the churchyard with, in the foreground, the Celtic cross memorial to the fifth Earl of Portsmouth.

now serves as a vestry. Piercing the wall between the chapel and chancel is a monument to Robert Oxenbridge (died 1574). Large with recumbent effigies, and at the sides, kneeling children. All of this is set in some typical classical period decoration, geometrical patterns and Ionic columns etc.

Outside, the churchyard is somewhat overgrown. On the north side a large cross, set in memorial to the Fifth Earl of Portsmouth. The view across paddocks with fine groups of horses, to estate cottages is particularly pleasing. To the north on its ridge can be seen the chimneys and roofs of what remains of

Hurstbourne Park. The larger part of what was an exceedingly large mansion, was demolished in 1965. The house had been designed in a Neo-Jacobean style in 1894 by Beeston and Burmester. Their house had replaced a very fine James Wyatt house, which had been burnt down in 1870. In the eighteenth century the pleasure grounds at Hurstbourne had been amongst the finest in the country. Even today although all the formal eighteenth-century grandeur has been swept away, the magnificent planting of trees in the ensuing two hundred years, has led to the present magnificent scenery.

Longparish – Thatches and tiled cottages.

Longparish

Some writers have referred to this particular stretch of the River Test as being the most beautiful countryside in the whole of the country. Whilst not going to that extreme, I will agree to it being of outstanding natural beauty, (my personal preferences would place a number of other Hampshire localities at least on a par). At something approaching three miles in length, the village lives up to its name and is a text book example of linear settlements, joining to form one large village. The church which is dedicated to St Nicholas, is situated in the former hamlet of Middleton. It dominates the village scene with its three stage

Perpendicular tower. The tower is built in a chequer flint and stone pattern. In one corner is a prominent stair turret and very large buttresses. The majority of the church dates from the earliest years of the thirteenth century, and although very substantially restored in 1853, retains much of the shape and architectural style of the original. Further large scale restorations were undertaken in 1958 and most recently between 1984 and 1989.

Internally, one outstanding feature of note is the Hawker window in the north aisle. It is unusual, not for its being a memorial to a young First World War officer (Major Lanoe George Hawker VC

DSO RFC, died 1916 aged 25), but in its unusual depiction of a primitive early air field and aircraft in the background of the window.

Mention of his family name leads to another memorial in the church, to perhaps the most famous member of the Hawker Family, namely Col Peter Hawker, whose sporting prowess with a rod and gun, have been made internationally famous by the publication of his diaries. He lived in the village from 1809 to his death in 1853.

Mottisfont – St Andrew's Church.

Mottisfont

This is the Test valley at its most mature, the River Test in two distinct and wide arms, is shortly joined by the River Dun. Well wooded countryside drops down towards the river. The parish is large, with clusters of agricultural buildings, farms and cottages built along the B3084. The real village which is actually very small, nestles around the edges of the great house, Mottisfont Abbey.

Mottisfont – View of the village.

The house and gardens are now the property of the National Trust. The houses of the village range from delightful Victorian estate cottages to very substantial Georgian houses. As with so many Hampshire villages the range of vernacular styles and materials is comprehensive. Well kept lawns, gardens and mature trees, put the finishing touches to this jewel of a village. The church sits at the eastern end of the village. Its setting up a small lane complete with attendant thatched cottages and seemingly growing out of the sloping churchyard, is wonderfully peaceful. Dedicated to St Andrew the entrance through the west end, which is surmounted by a shingle spire, is dramatic. A series of steps drop down abruptly to

Mottisfont – Eighteenth-century gravestone in the churchyard.

the nave. The church reveals mostly fourteenth and fifteenth-century work, but the single most impressive architectural feature is the Norman chancel arch. The chancel is justly famous for its wealth of fifteenth-century stained glass, more in fact than any other church in Hampshire. There is also a good late sixteenth-century monument in the chancel. The nave has a working clock mechanism dating from the seventeenth century.

It is however, the Gardens and house that make up Mottisfont Abbey, that people travel to see. The site started life as an Augustinian Priory, being founded in 1201. It never achieved the status of an Abbey and indeed for most of its existence, struggled to survive. It was nearly suppressed in 1494 but managed to hang on until its suppression in 1536. At this point the estate was purchased by Lord Sandys, who quickly converted the buildings into a house. The nave became the main body of the house along with the lower stage of the crossing tower. The north front reveals more of the monastic origins, than the much more famous south front, which was refaced in brick in the 1740s. The canted bays which form short

wings are indications of where the cloister ranges stood. The western one, still has a well preserved thirteenth-century cellarium. The eastern range which housed the Chapter house has survived in part, buried in the present fabric. Throughout the house parts of the original fabric have been exposed, revealing how much of the building still exists. Internally however, the most important room by far is the Drawing Room. It was one of the last major works by one of the great British artists of the twentieth century, Rex Whistler. Very theatrical, painted drapes and an urn with smoke rising from it, a masterpiece of *tromp-l'oeil* work.

Above one of the painted cornices is a depiction of a paint pot complete with brushes. It is a real *tour de force* and was undertaken between the years 1938 and 1939.

The gardens range from the sweeping lawns and mature trees which run down to the river, to the extensive walled gardens which house the National Collection of Old Fashioned Roses.

Nether Wallop

This is the southernmost and largest of the three Wallop villages – Over, Middle and Nether Wallop which line the Wallop Brook, which eventually joins the River Test just above Bossington. With the adjoining villages, the Wallops run for over three miles along the banks of the clear chalk stream. Over Wallop at the other end of the valley has a truely remarkable amount of thatched cob walls and is really the place in Hampshire to see this regional speciality.

Nether Wallop has survived surprisingly untouched by any large scale developments or infill. Its unspoilt charms led to its becoming part of the Miss Marple television detective series. The village is once again dominated by thatch and half timbering, but as with so many other Hampshire villages this is only half the story with a whole range of periods, styles and materials employed. There is the particularly stunning juxtaposition of half timbering, whitewashed infill, thatched

Nether Wallop – St Andrew's Church.

Nether Wallop – Corrugated iron and thatch, the range of vernacular styles in the village.

Nether Wallop – St Andrew's Church and pyramidal mausoleum to Dr Francis Douce, who died in 1760.

roofs, next to a corrugated iron former chapel which is complete with decorative wooden bargeboards.

The church is set on a sloping ridge, almost at the end of the village. Its position affords a particularly beautiful

Nether Wallop – Detail of the corrugated iron building.

view from the east, with the stream in the foreground and the sloping hillside into which the church is set.

St Andrew's Church has a complex architectural history and has a large number of very interesting features. The original Saxon church was a fairly ambitious cruciform structure, not dissimilar to Breamore. Its chancel arch was originally painted with a large and ambitious depiction of *Christ in Majesty* with four attendant angels. Although the later Norman chancel arch destroyed most of the scene, two angels and the tip of the mandorla (the oval frame) survived this and subsequent ravages to give us an all too brief and rare glimpse of eleventh-century painting. Returning to the

architectural development, the Normans expanded the size of the church adding a south aisle and extending the length of the chancel. In the thirteenth century a west tower was added, as well as a north aisle, transepts and chancel aisles. The fourteenth century saw the nave heightened and clerestory windows added. In the fifteenth century the chancel was altered once more, with its lengthening and widening. In the seventeenth and eighteenth centuries there was much repairing including the rebuilding of the west tower after its collapse in 1704. This accounts for its squat appearance as well as the plain corner pinnacles.

In 1845 there was a major reordering of

Nether Wallop – A perfect example of a Hampshire half-timbered, thatched cottage.

the church, and extensive repairs. All of these periods have left their mark in what is a very complex building history. Besides the remnants of the *Christ in Majesty*, there are a number of other fragments of wall paintings, the *Sabbath Breakers, St George and the Dragon,* and *St Nicholas.* These are all dated to the late fourteenth or early fifteenth century. Another unique object in the church, is the only known surviving mediæval brass of a Prioress, Mary Gore. She was the Prioress of Amesbury and died in 1436. She was buried in the church in the centre of the nave. There is also the ghostly outlines of

another former very large and outstanding brass memorial to an unknown Bishop. Only the matrix survives but it reveals a very large figure of a bishop wearing his mitre and holding a crozier. All of this is set under an ornate canopy, above which are two shields. All of this is set in a further architectural border. It is dated to the fourteenth century. That such a small village country church should come to hold the bodies and memorials of two such important religious figures is a mystery. One further strange fact about the church, is that here in deepest rural Hampshire, the Advowson, or right to present the Vicar has since 1133 been held by the Dean and Chapter of York Minster. This right was granted to them by Henry I. Immediately outside of the church, almost against the west tower is a very large stone pyramid which is topped by a flambeau. It is the tomb of Francis Douce whose wealth and eccentricity were well known.

Within the parish boundaries, lies the huge bulk of Danebury Hill. It is crowned by the massive earthworks of a large and powerful Iron Age hill-fort. This is the most comprehensively explored hill-fort in Britain having been the scene of eighteen seasons excavations under the leadership of Professor Barry Cunliffe.

St Mary Bourne – St Peter's Church tower and the neighbouring St Peter's cottage.

St Mary Bourne

High up in the north-west corner of the county, the village, which includes the northern extensions of Swampton and Stoke, is a text book example of a linear

settlement pattern along either side of the Bourne Rivulet. The stream eventually joins the River Test some two miles further south, just below Hurstbourne Priors. The

St Mary Bourne – The listed table tombs in St Peter's Churchyard.

St Mary Bourne – Summerhaugh Cottage.

St Mary Bourne – The view south below the Malt House.

valley has been continuously inhabited since the Iron Age. The southern approach to the village is very dramatically staged, with the brick arches of the Victorian railway viaduct, which carries the main London Waterloo line to the West, acting as a visual full stop.

Immediately to the north, lie the extensive watercress beds of Vitacress. A Hampshire agricultural speciality, these beds are supposedly the largest in Europe.

The gently curving street with its many thatched cottages, has at its centre the church of St Peter with its charming churchyard, complete with a very picturesque group of nine table tombs which are listed in their own right by the local borough council. The church itself sits at right angles to the road, with the west tower almost against the road. Of the original Norman church, little survives and what is seen now is largely of the late twelfth century. The large chancel dates from the fourteenth century, when the Wyke aisle was enlarged. The fabric of the church was restored in the 1850s at the expense of the Earl of Portsmouth. Chief amongst its treasures is the large and magnificent black Tournai marble font. It has carved on its sides, Norman arcading,

St Mary Bourne – The view north above Summerhaugh Cottage.

doves and vine leaves with bunches of grapes. It is the largest of the Tournai marble fonts in England, and as has already been said, it is one of four in Hampshire, and only nine in England. Nearby in a display case is a copy of a

Vinegar Bible. It dates from 1717 and is so called because of the replacement of the word vineyard by the mis-print vinegar, in the chapter heading of the Gospel of St Luke, Chapter Twenty. Set into the wall of the Wyke chapel is the recessed tomb of a knight, probably of Sir Roger des Andelys of Wyke Manor. The archetypal cross-legged figure of a knight although badly worn dates from *c.*1300. The church possesses many other features and fixtures of interest and more than repays a visit.

The church is situated just to the north of the spot where the ancient Roman road, known as the Portway and which ran from Silchester to Old Sarum, crossed the Bourne. Today the route is followed, on the western side of the valley, by a strikingly straight public footpath.

A slight distance to the north is set the village square, formed by the confluence of a number of roads. On the right-hand side, set in the garden of Treston Cottage, is a Victorian lamp standard, set up to commemorate Queen Victoria's Diamond Jubilee in 1897.

Just after the Bourne is crossed by a small bridge, which affords a new set of views, is on the left-hand side, a group of three cottages under one continuous thatched roof. The middle cottage, known as Hansdale is a very rare survival of a fifteenth-century timber cruck-framed cottage. Slightly further down on the opposite side are the flint and brick almshouses or Holdway Cottages. These were built in 1862 and a centrally positioned stone plaque records "In Memorium Robert Holdway 1862." He established a charity to help women in need who were over fifty-five years of age, who lived in the parish.

A major part of the charm of St Mary Bourne lies in its visual appeal. The way that the B3048, which is also the main street of the village, follows it seems, every curve and nuance of the Bourne Rivulet. This for considerable lengths runs adjacent to the road, before disappearing off behind a row of cottages only to reappear further on. The cottages and larger houses for their part also mirror these bends in the road and stream and, with the large range of styles and periods represented make for an ever changing series of views. Indeed the village has a wide range of building materials employed from brick, through chalk and cob with thatched roofing (which is a Hampshire speciality) to timber, flint and stone. This picture is completed by the ever present valley sides which close right in around the central part of the village, before opening out slightly before Stoke and then widening out gradually (although it can never be called a wide valley), once more as the valley rises towards Hurstbourne Tarrant.

Wherwell

For me this is the pick of those delightful villages which line the Test valley between Whitchurch in the east and Stockbridge to the west. Historically it was the seat of one of the most important and ancient of this country's nunneries. Founded by the Saxon Queen Elfrida, who after the death of her husband Edgar (the first King of all

England), was supposed to have had a fit of guilt about how she had been been a willing party in the murder of her first husband Ethelwold, and indeed later on, her stepson Edward (978) at Corfe Castle in neighbouring Dorset, to allow her son Ethelred the Unready to become King. Her first husband had been murdered in a 'hunting accident' in nearby Harewood Forest. The location is still known as

Wherwell – The quintessential Hampshire cottages, arguably the most famous row of thatched, half-timbered cottages in the county.

Wherwell – Thatched cottages by the River Test.

Wherwell – St Peter and the Holy Cross Church.

'Deadman's Plack'. That such a woman would ever have such a fit of conscience is debatable, but the fact remains that her setting up a nunnery at Wherwell set the village on its way. Today virtually nothing remains of the nunnery, and its site is partially covered by The Priory a dignified early nineteenth-century white mansion. It has a Tuscan porch and a cupola surmounting the roof. Jealously guarding its privacy, it was in 1988 sold and its contents auctioned.

The village slopes up from the river with the road running down to the church being full of white painted half-timbered thatched cottages. The church of St Peter and Holy Cross, having been totally rebuilt in 1858 by William Woodyer, perhaps lacks some of the charm expected

Wherwell – Mediæval monster heads from the corbel table of the original church and incorporated into the Victorian Iremonger family mausoleum, situated in the churchyard.

of such a picturesque and historic village. However his style and touch certainly led to an unusual building with some wilful breaking of architecturally correct vocabularies. From the old church relatively few objects were saved. These include an early fifteenth-century monument to a nun, some Saxon carved blocks and the tomb of Sir Owen West (died 1551). Some carved mediæval heads of monsters which came from the corbel table of the old church now decorate the Iremonger family Victorian mausoleum.

One final note about Wherwell is the mediæval story of its Cockatrice. This was a composite creature which had the head of a cock, the wings of a duck and a dragon's tail. It is supposed to have come into being by being hatched from an egg by a frog incubating the egg in a dark cellar. In the story it of course had a prediliction for human flesh. It had the ability to kill anything by simply looking at it. It was eventually killed, by being cornered in its lair, and subjected to its own stare by seeing itself in a mirror.

Northern Hampshire

On its western side, high chalk downs, tumble across the Wiltshire and Berkshire border. The downs in this area are massive and brooding. It is a region of small settlements. From this area, Ashmansworth and Crux Easton, have been chosen. The A34 acts as a good divider, its near north/south axis separates the high chalk downs from the lower but no less impressive chalk ridge, which includes Watership Down as it heads eastward. Below this scarp sit a string of pretty villages and towns, including Burghclere, Kingsclere, and Echinswell. To the north of this scarp, the land drops into the clays and heathlands of the Thames and Kennet valleys. This area was the site of the Romano-British regional capital of Calleva Atrebatum, modern day Silchester. The present settlement is someway to the west of the ancient town.

On the Berkshire border, Tadley, is the only reasonably sized urban landscape. To the south, the very large modern urban development of Basingstoke, has made a massive impact on the landscape. Yet almost perversely, due to the high railway embankment, the historically important village of Old Basing, has survived, right under the nose of Basingstoke. To the east and the border with Surrey and Berkshire, the urban development is almost continuous, from Yately, through Farnborough, Aldershot and Fleet. This is an area of heathland and pines, more akin to neighbouring Surrey. The geology is largely composed of Tertiary sand and gravels. Along the edge of the chalk, the sand and gravels are overlaid by a band of London Clay. These three geological belts meet at one of Hampshire's best villages, Crondall.

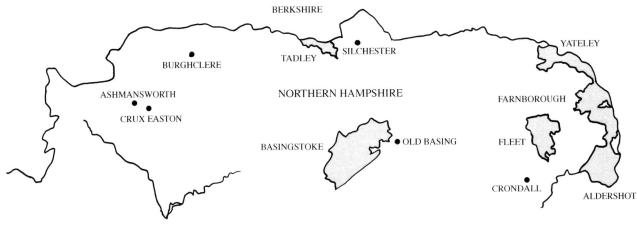

Ashmansworth

Set in very high remote chalk downland, the village of Ashmansworth is apparently the highest mediæval village on chalk anywhere in England. That fact alone would warrant an entry in this sample of Hampshire villages. It does however possess a number of attractions besides. It is a classic linear village, very long, with the village pub situated at the convergence of three lanes. The settlement is never more than one or two buildings deep. The buildings themselves are well spaced with the usual Hampshire range of vernacular styles. The church is the main feature to visit in Ashmansworth. Dedicated to St James, it is some considerable distance out of the centre. Don't lose your nerve as you plunge down a narrow lane heading south, but at the sign for Church Farm turn right and you will soon see the church in front of you. At the time of my last visit, the church was actually closed and covered in scafolding and plastic sheeting. The roof had been completely removed to allow a complete replacement. The church is not particularly large with a small nave and chancel dating from the Norman period. There is a brick south porch dating from 1694.

Internally the small Norman chancel arch has on either side the remains of once extensive wall paintings dating from the twelfth century. In the brick porch is a small exquisitely designed and engraved window, by Laurence Whistler, in memorial to Gerald Finzi and English music. Finzi lived in Ashmansworth from 1937 until his death in 1956. His gravestone is nearby, itself an important work of art, by Reynolds Stone.

Returning to the village, if you take the road to Faccombe or the road to East Woodhay you will be rewarded with exhilarating views and rapid falls and climbs, as the road follows the rapidly changing contours.

Burghclere

Burghclere is the middle straggling village of a group of three possessing the same name, Old Burghclere to the south and Burghclere Common to the north. Within the village of Burghclere itself, it is to one particular building that one's attention should be drawn. Next to the bridge over the long disused railway line, is the Sandham Memorial Chapel. Now in the possession of the National Trust, it consists of a nondescript oblong box with, at each side equally inoffensive low neo Georgian single-storey cottages, (designed by Lionel Pearson). Nothing prepares you for the contrast of the interior. The chapel itself was built as a memorial to Lieut H.W.Sandham and was commissioned by Mr and Mrs J.L.Behrend. Inside, the walls are covered in a series of nineteen scenes painted by Stanley Spencer.

They depict scenes from the Macedonian campaign and were painted between 1927 and 1932. There is nothing else like them in Britain let alone Hampshire and rank as a national if not internationally important artistic treasure. The chapel itself can be seen from the A34 and the ubiquitous brown National Trust signs leave you in no danger of missing the chapel.

Crondall – The Plume of Feathers pub.

Crondall

Situated in the north-eastern corner of the county, it is situated west of the alarmingly growing suburban expansion of Fleet, Farnborough, Aldershot and nearby Farnham, which is just over the Surrey border. Its present completely rural aspect set in rolling countryside, the chalk downs to the south and west, the heathlands of which so much of this part of north-east Hampshire are composed and finally a belt of clay. The geological diversity is reflected in the variety of materials used in

the village. The village slopes down the hill from the large and imposing church of All Saints. It is both impressive, externally and internally. Known locally as 'The Cathedral of North Hampshire', this is indicative of the impressive scale.

The site was certainly in use as a church from as early as the reign of King Alfred, although only the Saxon font remains today from the earliest period. The church's unusual external appearance is a result of the clay belt which runs through the parish being insubstantial enough to support the massive Norman stone church. The visual impact of the vast buttresses, which are dramatically evident on the south side, and which were built in 1556 in attempt to shore up the church and the large central Norman tower which was built over the chancel. It was all to come to a head in 1642 when a larger bell frame was inserted in the tower plus the reroofing of the tower in lead. The additional weight meant that by 1657 the drastic measure of demolishing the tower to save the rest of the church was undertaken. Interestingly enough the churchwardens were sent on a tour of the country to examine other towers and find a suitable model on which to base their new tower. The present brick tower, was built in 1659 and modelled on the now demolished tower of Battersea in London. The old stair turret of the former tower was retained and used as a means of access to the new tower. This resulted in the curious wooden bridges connecting the two structures.

Internally the nave is of massive Norman construction. Large piers carrying equally massive round arches. Above these are fine examples of transitional clerestory windows. The imposing chancel arches with good dog tooth decoration lead the eye to the two bay chancel with its vaulted roof. The east end windows are replacements put in during the restoration by Sir G.G.Scott in 1871. This swept away the box pews, galleries and the later mediæval east window. There are a number of interesting monuments and artefacts. These include the fourteenth-century brass to a rector, Nicholas de Kaerwent, and in the north

Crondall – All Saints' Church, the sixteenth-century brick tower.

transept a small needlework sampler depicting the design of a Roman mosaic pavement from a nearby villa. It was first uncovered in 1817 and has been subsequently destroyed. It consisted of guilloche bordered octagons, framing flowers and urns. The church is set in an extensive graveyard.

From the church the village slopes down hill, with the usual range of vernacular styles represented. There are a number of good eighteenth-century houses. Not surprisingly with its proximity to Surrey and being positioned on a belt of clay, there are a good number of tile hung houses. Brick predominates throughout the village. At the foot of the hill, the Plume of Feathers pub reveals its mediæval origins, the main portion of the building being jettied. The half timbering is admirably set off by the warm brick work. The streets all possess gentle curves which accentuate and highlight the homely character of the vernacular architecture of which Crondall is justifiably famed.

Crux Easton – St Michael's Church, a delightful Georgian box dating from 1775.

Crux Easton

Barely a couple of miles to the south-east of Ashmansworth, lies the tiny village of Crux Easton. Its claim to inclusion lies in its lost glories, connections with famous people, a delightful Georgian church and a unique surviving working windpump.

Firstly the church. This sits at the end of a long dead end road, the village if it can be called as such has the greatest concentration of buildings nearby. A group of cottages, some farm buildings, the church and a large house which was

Crux Easton – The windpump – a unique survival in Hampshire.

once the rectory. The long disappeared manor house was home to the Lisle family in the eighteenth century. In particular one Edward Lisle, who was a friend of the poet Alexander Pope. Lisle had twenty children, nine of them were daughters, who built a grotto which Pope immortalised in verse:

Here, shunning idleness at once and praise,
This radiant pile nine rural sisters raise;
The glittering emblem of each spotless dame,
Clear as her soul and shining as her frame;
Beauty which nature only can impart,
And such a polish as disgraces Art;
But fate disposed them in this humble fort,
And hid in desserts what would charm a Court.

Long vanished, the grotto is remembered by the woods still known as Grotto Copse.

The present church of St Michael replaced a Norman structure, which had probably become virtually ruinous by the time of its demolition in 1775. The present building is largely as it was built, with only some minor Victorian 'improvements'. A simple brick box with an apsed east end. The windows which have arched heads have emphasised brick keystones. These windows are clear lit. There is a small wooden porch. Inside, the sense of simplicity is continued with, by the door, a finely carved (probably Italian) marble font. The apse has a good marble pavement. The panelling around the apse, the lectern and the pulpit all date from *c.*1775.

Across the lane from the church, the former schoolhouse has been converted into a private dwelling. The former rectory, had as its final religious occupant, the Reverend Charles de Havilland. He was rector from 1897-1921. His son Geoffrey would go on to found the famous aircraft firm. Indeed he flew frequently from the village. The house served briefly at the end of the war as a home for Sir Oswald Mosley and his family.

As you leave the village, the first crossroads you come too will reveal, if you look through the gate into a field on your right, a low building with a windpump next to it. Looking for all the world like something from a view of the American West or the Australian Outback, it is unique in Hampshire. Because of the height at which Crux Easton is situated, getting water has always presented some sort of problem. A very deep bore was dug and a wind pump installed to pump the water into a nearby reservoir.

Old Basing

Despite being hemmed in to the north by a high, and in its own right, impressive railway viaduct, with the constant rush of trains along it, it is this embankment which has stemmed the complete encroachment by neighbouring Basingstoke. Stand in the churchyard or atop the ruins of Basing House and the tower block skyline is ever present, less than a mile away.

The village is still dominated by both the physical and atmospheric presence of Basing House. Once the largest private dwelling in Tudor England. Home to the

Old Basing – Seventeenth and eighteenth-century cottages opposite the ruins of Basing House.

Old Basing – The present entrance to the ruins of Basing House.

Lord High Treasurer, it was the scene of the Civil War's longest siege, which lasted from May until November 1644 and again in 1645 from July until October 14, when the final battle was led by Oliver Cromwell himself.

The ruins themselves are fairly extensive and are complicated to follow. A visit to the exhibition and excellent video, first, is recommended. Another particularly fine feature of the grounds are the magnificently restored, formal knot gardens. Having been virtually destroyed during the siege, the site was subsequently made into a garden and then during the nineteenth century, a canal was cut through part of the site.

Across the road from the site stands the substantial and very impressive tithe barn.

Between the ruins and the church, the village displays good examples of a range of cottages and houses in vernacular styles dating from the seventeenth to the twentieth centuries.

At the opposite end of the village, the church of St Mary, sits on a bank, acting as a foil to the ruins at the western end of the village. It is a large, mainly fifteenth century Perpendicular building which because of the large scale damage caused during the Civil War, had very extensive restoration work, post 1645. The church was very heavily restored by T.H.Wyatt in 1874. Internally there is evidence of the original Norman foundation. Apart from two Norman arches the church is completely Perpendicular or later.

Not surprisingly the church is full of monuments to the Paulet family, the ancestral lords of the manor and owners of Basing House. These are gathered together in the north and south chapels which sit either side of the chancel. These date from as early as 1492 and run through to the seventeenth century. There is also a monument by Flaxman to the Sixth Duke of Bolton, who died in 1794.

Silchester - The church of St Mary the Virgin.

Silchester – The Roman town today, with the city wall visible on the distant tree line.

Silchester

It is not to the modern settlement with its Calleva Arms, large green and houses set back behind high fences, that one's attention is drawn. But drive east from the village through a maze of lanes. Every now and then a glimpse of rubble masonry, then a stretch of higher wall with courses of stone built in amongst the flint

Silchester – The Roman amphitheatre.

Silchester – The Roman walls of Calleva Atrebatum with the bell turret of the church of St Mary the Virgin just visible.

is travelling. Approximately eighty acres enclosed as an irregular shaped polygon, which today is gently undulating farmland.

Only one building now stands within the Roman City. This is the church of St Mary the Virgin. It consists of a nave with a bell turret at the west end, aisles and a chancel. It is mostly of the thirteenth century with some fourteenth-century work in the south aisle. Features of interest include a Perpendicular screen, traces of mediæval wall painting and an eighteenth-century pulpit, which has a tester over it which is dated 1639. In the south aisle in the ogee headed tomb recess, is a fourteenth-century effigy of a lady wearing a wimple. The church is set in a small churchyard with only a small number of buildings nearby, to keep it company. Otherwise you are left to the solitude of the long empty Roman city and the mute testament of its crumbling walls.

Nearby to the north-east is the well preserved Roman amphitheatre.

and rubble infill. It is to the Silchester of the Romans, Calleva Atrebatum that one

Central Hampshire

A rather artificial division, which covers four downland villages, all situated on the central chalklands of Hampshire. An area of intensive agriculture, it is dotted with small settlements. A quiet region, its peace is punctured by the crossing of the region by the M3 motorway, the A30, A303, A33 and A34 trunk roads. As if this was not enough, the main London to Southampton railway, also runs in close proximity to these roads. One of the villages represented, East Stratton, started life as an estate village. Chilton Candover, is a good example of a deliberate act of depopulation in the sixteenth century. Micheldever and Stoke Charity, are both small, with outstanding architectural surprises.

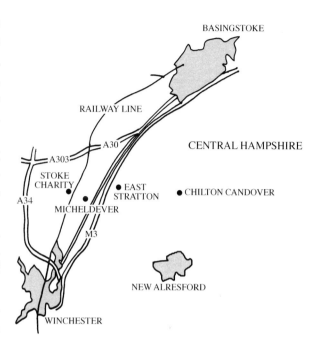

Chilton Candover

This is the middle village of the group of 'Candovers', the others being Preston and Brown Candover. This is a particularly wide rolling agricultural valley, with the area around Chilton Candover being particularly 'parklandesque', clumps of trees, and fine individual specimen trees, dotting the landscape. Set in this landscape are a scatter of cottages and more substantial farmhouses which comprise the village of Chilton Candover.

Besides the undeniable beauty of the landscape, Chilton Candover has one other surprise – the 'Buried Church' of St Nicholas. It is positioned some distance up the valley slope, and was once surrounded by various dwellings and a manor house, judging by the number of possible settlement platforms, ridges and other man-made features in the surrounding fields. The village did indeed date from the mediæval period and but for the vagaries of one man, would in all probability be yet another picture postcard setting today. It was in 1562 that a man named John Fisher bought the manor, and proceeded to demolish the village, scattering the population. This was an all too common occurrence in the Elizabethan period, with land being

Chilton Candover – The view across the valley from the churchyard of 'the buried' church of St Nicholas.

enclosed and sheep being put into pasture. The so called 'Buried Church' is in fact, the partially sunken crypt of the former church of St Nicholas, which was demolished in 1878. The church was then forgotten about for some fifty years, until the then rector was related a story by an old man in the parish, of playing in this crypt. He uncovered the crypt and cleared it out in 1925. Today a modern set of steps enter the crypt some way along, so that the original dimensions of thirty-two feet are no longer covered in. What is left is a sizeable vaulted room which finishes in an apse. Light is, and was, provided by a series of tiny lancet windows. These were set at the original ground level. In the vaulted section are a number of stone coffin lids and a Norman font. The crypt is set in a now largely empty graveyard, which is bounded by a flint wall.

The view back down the valley, is breathtaking, very remote and peaceful. Across the road in the valley bottom, starts an impressive avenue of yew trees, which stride out purposefully for some considerable distance, seemingly starting and going nowhere. If there once was a house at the end of the drive, it has left neither trace or record.

East Stratton – Some of the five pairs of estate cottages designed by George Dance the Younger, in the first decade of the nineteenth century.

East Stratton

This is yet another classic estate village, this time dating from the the late eighteenth and early nineteenth century. The village served the, 'Big House', in this case Stratton Park. The house was a spectacular Georgian classical pile complete with a very large and impressive central Doric portico designed by George Dance the Younger in 1803. He was also responsible for the dramatic alterations to neighbouring Micheldever Church. The house was demolished with the exception of the portico, and replaced by a completely incongruous modern house between 1963 and 1965, (designed by Stephen Gardiner and Christopher Knight). An act of wanton barbarity or a brave step forward, the individual must decide.

The village is a long string of cottages and buildings along two roads. The centre of the village at the crossroads by the church is particularly pretty. The thatched cottages which stand out are five pairs of two-storey, single-bay cottages, each with an attached side porch. These were also designed by George Dance the Younger.

The church was built between 1885-90 in a particularly hard and uncompromising Victorian style by Sir Thomas Jackson. He had built the magnificent church at nearby Northington, altogether in a different class by comparison.

The village today is blighted by the noise of the M3 which is less than a mile away and even closer to Stratton Park. Indeed the motorway construction caused the severing of a number of the gate lodges from the rest of the park.

Micheldever – A view of the village.

Micheldever – The church of St Mary the Virgin, with the octagonal nave, of 1806, by George Dance the Younger.

Micheldever

If you take the turning, signposted to Micheldever, from the A33 you find yourself driving down a straight road bordered by exceptionally wide grass verges and rows of trees. It feels for all the world as if you have entered the drive to a large private stately home. There is in fact only a farm halfway down on the right-hand side. It does however act as a trumpet call for the village of Micheldever. Not particularly large, the village pos-

Micheldever – Shillingbury Cottage dating from 1463.

Micheldever – Black and white, thatched half-timbered, and white painted brick cottages.

sesses a number of memorable groups of cottages, a Victorian school (1870) complete with clock tower and a singularly different church set in a well wooded yard.

The church of St Mary The Virgin is unlike any other in Hampshire. Externally it has a fine Perpendicular sixteenth-century west tower built of stone, possibly brought from the site of Hyde Abbey in Winchester. The nave was rebuilt in 1806 due to the existing fabric being in such a poor condition. The architect chosen, George Dance, was at the time working on Stratton Park in neighbouring East Stratton. What he did was to say the least, highly unusual. In place of a standard nave rose a large brick octagon. It looks for all the world like something from an ancient Byzantine church and not the middle of deepest rural Hampshire! To the east of this is a normal conventional chancel which was rebuilt in 1881. Internally the church is dominated by the large octagonal nave which soars to a vaulted roof on very slender Gothic pillars. Six of the octagons' faces have lights which flood the nave with light and emphasise the darkness of the chancel. In the chancel are three monuments to members of the Baring family, the best dating from the Regency period, is reputed to be one of, if not the finest monuments by Flaxman.

Returning to the village the finest groupings of cottages are to the south of the church at a road junction which also possesses a small piece of triangular green, underneath a large tree, with seats grouped around its base. The cottages reveal timber construction and one dates from the second half of the fifteenth century.

Remains of a Roman Villa have been discovered in Micheldever Wood and are evidence of the long history of occupation in this particular location. Today with the A33 and M3 acting as a barrier to the south-east and the main London to Southampton railway line equidistant to the west, the village is affected by the roar of both traffic and trains but remains mercifully under-developed.

Stoke Charity

Only a few miles to the west of Micheldever, lies the tiny village of Stoke Charity. It sits close to the equally tiny River Dever (which eventually joins the River Test at Wherwell). It has the normal Hampshire mix of cottages and houses, built in the usual range of styles and materials. It is however the church at Stoke Charity which lifts the village above the ordinary. The church itself sits on its own to the east of the present village. It would seem that the village has gradually developed away from the church leaving it in its present isolated position.

The church is dedicated to St Mary and St Michael and as has been mentioned is set in a turfed churchyard surrounded by fields. It is small, constructed largely of flint and completely modest and unassuming. The fabric dates back to the Saxon period but is largely of Norman workmanship. Inside however is one of the largest and richest assemblages of monuments and fittings of any village church in Hampshire. There is a tomb chest to Thomas Wayte (died 1482), which has a Purbeck marble slab on the top, into which is set a brass of a knight complete with the scene of Christ rising from a coffin. The tomb chest of Thomas Hampton (died 1483) is set between the chancel and the Hampton Chapel. This too has a Purbeck marble top, into which are set the full length brasses of him and his wife. There are various inscriptions and a depiction of their eight daughters. Against the north wall of the chapel is the Jacobean tomb chest of Sir Thomas Phelipps (died 1626).

In the North Chapel is the tomb of John Waller (died 1526). This is positioned below a Tudor style canopy. Nearby on the floor is a badly damaged brass to Richard Waller (died 1551). The chapel's greatest treasure is however, the unique survival of a carving of the Mass of St Gregory. It was discovered in 1849 and placed here in 1900. In 1966 the remains of a thirteenth-century wall painting, depicting a male figure, were uncovered. A number of the windows contain numerous jumbled fragments of mediæval stained glass collected together.

The Itchen and its tributaries

Second in fishing reputation to the Test, the River Itchen, has its source, high up in the chalk downlands of central Hampshire. Its tributaries gather to the west of New Alresford and its course is westward towards the county town and one time national capital, Winchester. It then heads south through an increasingly urban landscape, to enter the sea, at Southampton Water. The villages chosen to represent this river valley, are clustered around its source, Cheriton, Tichborne, Northington and Avington. The region is intensively farmed, large fields slope down the sides of the chalk hills, with lush watermeadows, in the wide valley bottoms.

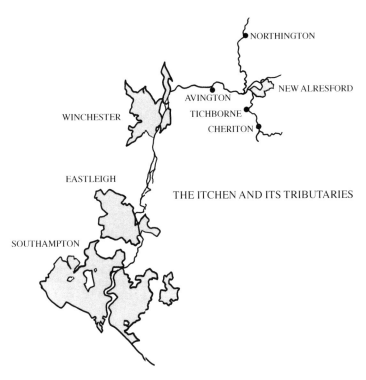

THE ITCHEN AND ITS TRIBUTARIES

Avington

Avington is a very small village, more a hamlet, a row of seven cottages which face across the road to the estate wall, the church and to Avington Park. It is the church, house and grounds which call for our attention. St Mary's Church was built between 1768 and 1771 at the expense of Margaret Marchioness of Caernarvon, who was the wife of the Third and last Duke of Chandos. She in fact died in 1768 before the completion of the church.

The mediæval church had long since disappeared before the decision to build the Georgian church. Externally it is a brick built three bay box, with crenellations. The tower is likewise built of brick, of three stages with again crenellations. The windows in each of the bays of the nave have arched heads and exaggerated keystones. The east window is a Venetian window. The doorways have a Gibbs style rustication. All this helps to

Avington – Avington Park, the recessed wooden portico.

arvon (died 1768) consists of an obelisk and two urns. The one to George Bridges (died 1751) consists of two pillars supporting a broken pediment. Beneath the pediment is a sarcophagus and an urn. Against the north wall of the sanctuary is a display case containing a Vinegar Bible dating from 1717. (For a full description of a Vinegar Bible please see the entry for St Mary Bourne.)

To the north of the church lies the house and grounds of Avington Park. The grounds sweep down to a branch of the River Itchen which then rejoins the other branch further down past the lake. With the landscaped ground rising gradually up towards the well wooded chalk slopes in a westerly direction, the aforementioned clear, wide and fast flowing River Itchen to the north, it is a veritable paradise. Underneath the shade of the many overhanging trees, large trout nonchalantly swim against the current. At one point the river is crossed by a graceful cast-iron bridge, dating from 1800, which is now the subject of a restoration appeal.

Between the house and the church which is surrounded by a dense thicket of trees, the ground is turfed, thus setting the house on a well-kept green lawn. The house itself is of brick and appears to date from the early eighteenth century. It does however mask earlier houses on the site dating from the very late sixteenth and early seventeenth centuries. The west front contains the most impressive external feature, the recessed portico. Rising the full height of the building, it consists of four giant Tuscan columns supporting a pediment, surmounted by three lead statues (Minerva, Juno and Ceres). All of the portico is constructed of wood and

give it the feel of a Georgian church of the earliest part of the eighteenth century and not some sixty years later. Internally the eighteenth-century interior is almost unaltered – very tall box pews, a three decker pulpit complete with tester above, surmounted by a dove, reredos and west gallery all built out of mahogany. There are wrought-iron communion rails and a marble baluster font. Along the north wall of the church, above the various pews are pegs for wigs. Hanging from the plain white barrel vaulted roof is a very elaborate brass chandelier of 1771.

There are three monuments of note, that of Margaret Marchioness of Caern-

painted a brilliant white, which on a bright sunny day really strikingly offsets it against the warm red brickwork. This part of the house has been attributed to the architect John James. On the southern side of the house, behind the central block, is the gently bowed library which adjoins a graceful mid nineteenth-century conservatory. This is joined to a matching conservatory by an open colonnade. Situated on the lawn opposite this is a spectacular fountain brought from London.

Internally the guided tour takes one through five splendid rooms all of which contain much of interest. These include the quite outstanding first floor Ballroom or Great Saloon, the Red Drawing Room and the Library. The house and grounds are open on most summer weekends and are a highly recommended visit.

Cheriton

Barely two miles south of Tichborne and closer to the source of the River Itchen, Cheriton is a very pretty nucleated village, set around a green, through which runs the infant River Itchen. The church of St Michael and All Angels, sits on a large artificial prehistoric mound. This means visually, the extreme length of the church

Cheriton – The church of St Michael and All Angels, on its prehistoric mound.

Left: Cheriton – Hampshire building materials stone, flint and brick.

Right: Cheriton – Hampshire building materials stone and flint.

can be appreciated and at the same time see how the builders of the church took full advantage of the sloping site. There is evidence of all periods of work from the Norman period onwards. It is largely however of the Early English style, with the chancel being extended both in the fifteenth and sixteenth centuries. The church suffered a disastrous fire in 1744, after which the church was restored over a period of two years. In 1879 the church was subject to a large scale Victorian restoration. Set into the walls of the porch either side of the entrance, complete with Norman shafts are two spherical triangles, which consist of six interlacing circular shapes. The middle therefore creates three further interlacing circles. No complete explanation has ever been given as to what they are and why they came to be set into the walls of the porch. Above each of

these are a pair of carved heads that were once set into the western wall of the churchyard. A walk around the outside of the church reveals in this one location, text book examples of the use of the local Hampshire building materials. This is especially true of the northern side of the tower, where combinations of brick, flint and stone blocks can be seen. The views from the top of the bank across the valley to surrounding downs is particularly good to the north-west. The village saw one of the bloodiest encounters of the Civil War, with the Battle of Cheriton in 1644. It took place just to the north-east below Cheriton Wood and marked the turning point in the war. The Roundheads scored a decisive victory over the Royalist forces. Over eight thousand men fought a pitched battle all day.

Northington

Geographically this is in the heart of the county. Set in rolling downland, the valley has a swift crystal clear tributary of the Itchen running through it. Lush watermeadows support large herds of cows. It is a village without a pub, without a post office or shop or village school. Its

houses are largely unmemorable – a mixture of former estate cottages, and more recent infill, especially bungalows. Its claim to recognition lies in it being home to one of the most remarkable buildings in Europe, The Grange. Designed by William Wilkins in 1817 (he

Northington – The church of St John the Evangelist.

designed The National Gallery in Trafalgar Square, London) a typical country house was transformed into an architecturally and archaeologically exacting example of Greek Doric architecture. In short, a massive ancient Greek temple set down amongst an outstanding English landscape garden setting. The fields with their sheep and cows, dotted with wind blasted Lebanon cedars, hillside plantations reflected in the serpentine lake, that the same small fast flowing stream has become. It is a setting of utter peace and solitude. On the many occasions I have been there I have had it to myself with only the sounds of animals and birds on the lake to break the silence.

The present state of the building now admirably administered by English Heritage, is that of a well maintained, gutted but roofed building. Only thirty years ago its sumptuous interiors were intact. Sixty years ago it was offered to the nation with its fabulous contents as a museum – an offer criminally rejected. Years of different owners and subsequent neglect meant that by the early 1970s its future was on a knife edge. Its owners wanted to demolish it by explosives. It became a *cause célèbre* of the infant Heritage lobby, and after tense often tortuous negotiations, it was saved at the eleventh hour. Even then it was still subject to further decay before the main portion of the house was saved. Today with its gaunt black hessian covered windows, it stands in splendid isolation, tucked away in its idyllic setting. Leaving, down what feels like an endless rutted and pot holed road, you pass a very impressive complex of buildings, closely surrounded by the 'Hampshire Weed', the Yew. Rising above the trees is a bell tower in a French Chateaux style. I presume this was the stable block for the Grange.

The Lords Ashburton (Baring Family) were not finished with building and on the hillside above most of the village, sits Northington's other architectural gem, its church (St John Evangelist) Designed by Sir Thomas Jackson, it is as fine an example of Late High Victorian Gothic revivalism that you can find. The sloping site has been cleverly manipulated to allow for the apsidal east end. The west end has a tall Somerset style Perpendicular tower, evidently added after Lady Ashburton had seen St John's Church at Glastonbury. Inside its High Victorian fittings are complete. A high level stone pulpit is reached by a stone spiral staircase set into the thickness of the wall.

Not surprisingly, the church is full of Baring family monuments and memorials, including one dated 1848 by Westmacott Jun., which is considered his masterpiece.

Tichborne

The village is scattered over the slopes of a spur of the chalk downs, and on down into the valley of the infant River Itchen. The lush watermeadows contrast with the large fields on the side of the downs. The church shows evidence of its Saxon origins in the stone pilaster strips and the small double splayed windows set in the

Tichborne – The monument to Richard Tichborne, who died in 1619, aged 18 months and two days. It is in the north aisle of Tichborne Church, and is unusual, in that it has and still does serve as a Roman Catholic chapel.

chancel walls. Most of the nave and chancel, dates from the twelfth and thirteenth centuries. The brick west tower dates from 1703. The north aisle which is packed with outstanding monuments to the Tichborne family, is very unusual in that it served and still does as a Roman Catholic chapel. The family remained steadfastly loyal to the Roman Catholic faith and also managed to retain their positions of eminence. The two major monuments are the splendid and moving alabaster figure of a young baby boy dressed in contemporary clothes. This is set under a simple arch. It is the monument to Michael Tichborne who died in 1619 aged eighteen months. The

outstanding monument is that to Sir Benjamin Tichborne (died 1621). Again of alabaster it depicts two recumbent figures (Sir Benjamin and his wife Amphillis). On the side of the tomb are finely carved depictions of their seven children. Over the tomb rises a cornice supported on two columns. Above this along the wall of the chapel are a series of family hatchments. The chapel is separated from the rest of the church by some good Elizabethan iron railings. The church also possesses amongst other features, a Norman font, Jacobean box pews and communion rails.

The village has had virtually no intrusive modern infill and what there has been blends in well with the surroundings.

Of particular note in the main street is the Old Post Office which dates from the earliest years of the seventeenth century. The Tichborne Arms at the bottom of the street on the right is a replacement of the original building which was burnt down in 1939. On the left-hand side opposite, the pub are three cottages, the middle one (Park View), has been the subject of detailed dendrochronological dating. This has established that the house dates from c.1480. It is also the best preserved Cruck-house in Hampshire. Opposite these cottages a road crosses the Itchen and heads towards Tichborne House. The present house dates only from 1803 and has a particularly fine porch which is carried on four Tuscan columns, and has a triglyph frieze. The house which has seven bays, is painted white and stands proudly in good grounds, which include a series of water features including a lake. On the south front of the house, a flight of stairs descends to the garden, with at the base, a pair of very elaborate oriental bronze ornamental features. The west side of the house has a chapel of three bays, which from the exterior is totally Georgian. I have never been able to get inside and can find no description of it. This side of the house is next to a very large oblong ornamental pond. The grounds are open on a very small number of days each year and are worth visiting.

The house, or to be strictly correct its Elizabethan predecessor, was the scene of the famous Tichborne Dole. A painting hanging in the house, painted by the Flemish artist Giles Tilburg shows the start of the distribution of the dole in 1670, set in front of the original Elizabethan mansion.

The legend starts in the thirteenth century, when the dying wife of Sir Roger Tichborne, one, Lady Mabella, asked her husband to organise a charitable bequest. He is supposed to have said, that he would grant each year, the equivalent amount of bread made from the corn growing in the area, which she could get round in a set period of time. Dying and too weak to walk she apparently crawled around a field which was twenty-three acres in size. As a result each year after that the Tichborne Dole was distributed to the families in the district.

The Meon Valley

Perhaps the least known of the Hampshire river valleys, the River Meon, starts its journey, seaward on the flanks of Butser Hill. It heads west, through the outstanding village of East Meon, with its truely magnificent church, until it reaches West Meon and a turn southwards. West Meon, besides its visual charms, has a number of notable connections and final resting places. At Warnford, the river traverses a little known eighteenth-century landscape garden before wending its way to the cluster of villages comprising, Exton, Corhampton and Meonstoke. A little further down at Droxford, the chalk scenery, gives way to a belt of London Clay. Close by is situated Soberton. The next village downstream, Wickham, is special, even by the standards of the Meon valley. Its square is a real surprise, a planning *tour de force*. As if the valley has not already served up a rich enough feast, the final word is given to Titchfield. Rapidly being surrounded by twentieth-century sprawl, the village possesses a number of fine points, including, the church and the ruins of an Abbey. After this the river meanders gently to the sea and Titchfield Haven.

The Meon valley below Soberton.

WEST MEON

WARNFORD

EAST MEON

EXTON

CORHAMPTON

MEONSTONE

DROXFORD

SOBERTON

WICKHAM

THE MEON VALLEY

FAREHAM

TITCHFIELD

A little way south of Exton and straddling the A32, the village would be rather anonymous but for its outstanding church.

Corhampton

Set on a small artificial bank, itself of considerable antiquity, stands a small two cell Saxon/Norman church which possesses no known dedication. The churchyard, equally small is dominated by an enormous yew tree. Inside, a number of features catch the eye, including the Victorian gallery, the Jacobean pulpit and the Saxon/Norman font. But it is in the chancel that the church's claim to fame lies. Large sections of the wall are covered in the twelfth-century wall painting depicting the story of St Swithun.

Droxford

Yet another bewitching village in the Meon Valley, it is unfortunately marred by the increasingly busy A32 rushing through the middle of the village, making one side of the village, and indeed what was once a large triangular green, and now largely a tarmaced car-park, almost cut off from the rest of the village. This centrally placed car-park is a good place to start a walk around the village. At this point the village slopes up either way, with a good range of largely Georgian cottages and more substantial houses, set back behind high walls, interspersed with thatched cottages. The A32 to the south curves gently, and at the same time as I have mentioned, slopes upwards. The White Horse Inn forms an integral part of this scene. Further up, more and more substantial houses, take over on either side of the road. Walking

back toward the centre of the village, the lane running off to the left, contains a Victorian police station, and further down a Victorian non-conformist chapel, which now serves as part of a garden centre. This part of the village is composed largely of Victorian and more recent infill. At the northern edge are a number of very modern executive developments.

The road north through the village, once again climbs and curves away from the centre. There are a number of fairly distinguished, largely Georgian houses, which continue for some considerable distance, before heading south and petering out in to larger buildings at the village edge. Returning to the centre and heading down towards the meadows and the River Meon, there are a number of large properties. The two main houses are

Droxford – St Mary and All Saints.

Droxford – The White Horse Inn.

the Rectory and the Manor House. The Manor House, which can be glimpsed through the fine iron railings, is a fine largely seventeenth-century house built of brick, with a particularly fine west front. Its walled gardens slope down almost to the river. Nearby is the Old Georgian Rectory which besides being the finest house in the village, (it is of five bays, with the centre three projecting and of local red and grey brick), was for part of the later stages of his life, home to Izaak Walton. His connection with Droxford, was because of his daughter being married to the rector.

The church is dedicated to St Mary and All Saints, and sits in a spacious churchyard full of trees. All this borders the meadows which stretch down to the river. Externally the dominant feature is the large west tower which was built in 1599. It has a prominent square stair turret and large buttresses. The windows and west door in the tower all reveal the Tudor date for building. On the north side, the nave roof slopes down over the aisle in an unbroken sweep, seemingly further emphasising the massiveness of the tower. On the southern side, an element of domesticity is introduced, with a series of eighteenth-century dormer windows added. Both the north aisle and the door

Droxford – The view southwards up the A32.

inside the Porch are Norman. The church internally is mainly of Norman workmanship, nave and chancel arch. The north aisle and chapel date from the twelfth century, with the south aisle and its chapel being added in the thirteenth century. The aisles and their chapels were rebuilt in the fourteenth century. Most of the fittings are nineteenth century, there are however seventeenth-century communion rails. There are a number of monuments from an equally wide range of periods.

Droxford reflects its locality, with a move from predominantly thatched cottages of half timbered or flint construction. Instead, reflecting the move from chalk downland into a clay rich area, there is an abundance of locally produced brick and tile. Some commentators have remarked, that it is a pity that so many of the buildings in the village are whitewashed, and thus hiding the mellow red and grey bricks. Once again it is up to the individual to make their mind up. Whatever the outcome of the aesthetic debate about the pros and cons of whitewashed houses versus natural colours, Droxford needs to be explored on foot to give up its secrets.

East Meon

If you drive in from the south over the flank of Butser Hill you are presented with a grandstand view of the valley of the infant River Meon. Nestling against the southern slope of Park Hill, is arguably one of the most impressive churches of

East Meon – Thatched cottages and the infant River Meon.

vernacular styles, from thatched cottages at the eastern end to the impressive Georgian house at the western end of the street. There is a memorial cross by the bridge with the view northwards past The George, the almshouses and some fine larger eighteenth-century houses, to the church set into the hillside, with the chalk down rising virtually sheer, immediately behind. In spring the churchyard is a riot of colour, filled with daffodils. Opposite the churchyard stands The Court House. A venerable survival from the mediæval period, its name reveals its former use. From here the Bishops of Winchester administered their vast estates in this area and from this period survives the large mediæval hall with finely carved corbels. Nothing really prepares you for the sense of both scale and

East Meon – Old Well Cottage.

Southern Britain. The village itself is built along and around a series of streams which form the River Meon. The centre of the village, which contains both pubs, is very photogenic, with a range of the feeling of a time warp as you step in from the terraced gardens into the hall, which rises clear to the mediæval rafters. All of this space is lit by tall clear lancets. The hall is adjoined by a rambling house

East Meon – The George Inn with the almshouses beyond.

East Meon – A general view of the centre of the village.

East Meon – All Saints Church, set into the side of Park Hill.

East Meon – The Court House, opposite the church.

– a mixture of a number of periods. The hall together with the gardens are open on a few occasions during the year and it is worth making a special effort to see it.

The church of All Saints, having made such a tremendous visual impact from afar, does not disappoint either close to or with the interior. Although much rebuilt, there is a fine Norman tower and west doorway to admire. Internally every period is represented, from Norman to Modern. Amongst its chief treasures are a magnificent black Tournai marble font, dating from the late eleventh century (one of only nine in Britain, of which four are in Hampshire), and a series of stained glass windows and altar furnishings by Sir John Ninian Comper, culminating in the magnificent East window of 1920. If it is open, take the opportunity to climb to the bell chamber. The church is blessed with a good peal of bells. Having ambled around the village, one further walk should be undertaken. Following the footpath signs through the churchyard, you quickly gain the steep grassy slopes of Park Hill. The effort is rewarded with a magnificent birds eye view of both the church and village.

Exton

This is perhaps scenically, one of the most dramatic parts of the Meon Valley with high chalk downs falling steeply to the valley floor. Exton is situated on the western side of the valley. At this point of the valley, three villages, namely Exton, Corhampton and Meonstoke are literally but a stone's throw apart. Approaching from over Beacon Hill, the valley is laid out below, Warnford and West Meon, visible to the north, and the three aforementioned villages directly below. Exton lies off the A32 and is secreted around a number of intersecting lanes.

Nothing particularly memorable, individually but overall, the charm of a range of vernacular styles in the cottages and more substantial houses. The church of St Peter and St Paul was rebuilt in the mid nineteenth century and rather like the village is not exceptional but homely. It was built using the local indigenous material – flint. The pub, The Shoe has a delightful garden which runs down to the fast flowing River Meon. In summer, the ducks will happily wander amongst the patrons searching for titbits.

Meonstoke

Barely a quarter of a mile away from Corhampton sits Meonstoke. The large church with its wooden capped tower, sits amongst water meadows. Along with the adjacent buildings the scene is particularly picturesque. Nearby is the very popular Bucks Head, which marks the beginning of a long rising street of mainly period houses with some modern infill. At the top of the rise is a small triangular green and an even longer street running southwards along a ridge above the valley bottom.

St Andrew's Church was built unusually close to the river and replaced an earlier Saxon church on the same site. It dates mainly from the twelfth century, and is largely of the Transitional style. The tower has its lower stage built from flint rubble and dates from the fifteenth century. The upper wooden stage, which gives the church such a distinctive outline was added in 1900.

Soberton

The village sits just over a ridge on the eastern side of the Meon valley, to the south-east of Droxford. The original part of the village is small in comparison to its near neighbour Droxford, and hugs either side of the road, thus producing a linear settlement pattern. More recent Victorian and modern development has taken place southwards at Soberton Heath. The centre of the village is around a green with the White Lion pub on one side and the church of St Peter and St Paul on another. The church dates mostly from the twelfth and thirteenth centuries. It was on

Soberton – The White Lion, on the village green, with the chalk downs beyond.

the site of an earlier Norman church. The west tower is a classic Hampshire village church tower, late Perpendicular with three stages, a large stair turret, with the construction being of flint and stone, laid in a chequer work pattern. At the top are set some good mediæval carvings, including that of a skull set between two heads, a key and a purse. Not surprisingly, the church has a wealth of features and details, including extensive traces of very early fourteenth-century wall painting in the south transept, box pews, seventeenth-century communion rails and the normal collection of Victorian fittings. There is also an outstanding mid eighteenth-century monument by Peter Scheemakers, to Thomas Lewis, who died in 1747. It depicts a sarcophagus which has cherubs at each end. On the sarcophagus is a bust.

On the other side of the green, and dominating the central part of the village, is the very large late nineteenth-century Soberton Towers. It was designed by its builder and owner, Colonel Charles Brome Bashford. Constructed of flint with stone dressings, the best view of its battlemented façades is to be gained when taking the road down into the Meon Valley. At a point on the bridge over the disused, and heavily wooded Meon Valley Railway cutting, can be seen part of the western façade of the house.

Titchfield – The view down East Street, showing the range of Georgian fronted houses.

Titchfield

Once a port, the village has miraculously survived the complete late twentieth-century infill of the surrounding countryside, as the inexorable development of all the space between Portsmouth and Southampton continues apace. The village itself lies to the south of the A27, which itself has been largely superseded by the M27, which now travels a parallel course less than a mile to the north.

The A27 does however split the village from the ruins of Titchfield Abbey. It was

Below: Titchfield – The view of St Peter's Church, from the northern side. The very impressive Perpendicular north aisle dominates the scene.

Titchfield – The view down Church Street.

Titchfield – The Bugle Hotel.

Bishop of Winchester. It was never a vast complex and would appear to have had a relatively uneventful history and was dissolved in 1537, having probably been little changed architecturally from its early thirteenth-century appearance. It was converted very quickly into a model Tudor courtyard mansion. The work was in fact complete by 1542. The nave of the church was converted into the main gatehouse, the east end and the central tower being demolished. The cloister was retained as a courtyard and the existing conventual buildings around it, converted or used as a ready made quarry of stone.

It became known as Place House and was the splendid home to Thomas Wriothesley, Earl of Southampton. It is thought that Shakespeare was a visitor to

an abbey of the Premonstratensian Order and was founded in 1232 by the then

Titchfield – The Queen's Head.

Titchfield – The view up East Street.

the place as the Third Earl was an important patron. The house itself remained in use until the latter part of the eighteenth century, when in 1781 it was demolished and much of the stone transported to nearby Delme Hall, to be incorporated in a splendid new mansion rising by the banks of Fareham Creek. What is left today is the very impressive, substantial, text book example of Tudor architecture, that comprises the gate-house. The four octagonal towers with good mullioned windows, stand to their full height. Either side of this a virtually blank curtain wall runs to smaller octagonal towers. The western one is surmounted by a particularly fine barley twist

Tudor brick chimney. Behind the gatehouse, the low walls and ground plan of the monastic buildings are laid out in the turf. There are also some good stretches of mediæval tiles exposed. The entrance to the Chapter House survives, albeit in a ruinous state, to reveal something of the graceful lines which the Abbey must have once possessed. The former refectory of the monastery, not surprisingly became the Great Hall of the house, but this is now reduced to little more than low walling. The entire site is set behind a high brick wall, with the outer areas of the enclosed courtyard being laid to turf, with various fruit trees. To the west of the abbey precinct, set in fields, is the former abbey tithe barn. Immediately to the south of the site, is the rather incongruously sited Titchfield Abbey Nurseries. Across the road are a few cottages, a pub and close by the River Meon, now in its final push to the sea at Titchfield Haven.

Returning to the village, it is of a fairly regular plan and was undoubtedly planned from the outset in the mediæval period. The square which is formed by the widening of the High Street is the centre of the village with most of its shops and pubs. Indeed the overwhelming sense of period which is given off at first glance is of Georgian brick houses of a range of sizes and shapes. These in all probability hide behind their brick façades the timber frames of much older houses. The square's two pubs are amongst its more impressive buildings. The Bugle Inn on the south side has two polygonal bay windows which rise through the full three storeys. Between these the segmental porch is carried on two pillars. The pub flies the Union flag proudly from the centre of its roof. On the western side of the square at the opposite end is the Queens Head. This too has bays and a central porch carried on columns, but is a storey less in height. Opposite this are a number of houses with fine Georgian pedimented doorcases.

The northern end of the High Street is brought to a good stop by a well proportioned brick, double bay windowed Georgian house, which also serves as an introduction to the slightly inclined East Street. This is lined on both sides by homely rather than impressive, largely Georgian housing. At the bottom a right turn down a relatively short side street leads you to the large churchyard and the church of St Peter. Coming into the churchyard from the north reveals the very fine Perpendicular north aisle, lit by four large three light windows. The chancel likewise reveals Perpendicular workmanship, although nowhere on the scale or quality of the north aisle. The west tower from this veiwpoint appears insignificant and topped by a low shingle spire. If you walk round to the west end or indeed arrive at the church having taken the short street down from the High Street, you are confronted by an altogether more interesting view of the tower. What is in front of you is in fact a very early (AD*c*.700) Anglo-Saxon west porch. There is a bonding course made of re-used Roman tiles and the original western doorway. It is with the exception of Breamore, which is two hundred years later, the single most important piece of Saxon work in Hampshire. Internally the Perpendicular north aisle floods this part of the church with light. The nave and chancel are basically thirteenth century, with the south aisle being a total Victorian rebuild. The adjacent south chapel or Southampton chapel was until the dissolution of the monasteries the property of the Abbey. It became a natural place for the Earls of Southampton to be interred. In 1989, the Victorian vestry and the west end of the south aisle were closed in and converted into a two floor group of vestries, meeting rooms, choir rooms etc. To say that this has been done sympathetically would be to understate the stark, and damaging visual impact upon the church. Indeed the totally different purpose of the rooms contained within, with their modern facilities do jar on the senses.

The Southampton chapel contains a number of monuments, but all are overpowered by the absolute monster sized, *tour de force* that is the monument to the First Earl and Countess of Southampton, (died 1551 and 1574 respectively) and their son the Second Earl. It was

Titchfield – A stretch of eighteenth-century wall, in West Street, which incorporates sheep knuckle bones.

executed in 1594 by Gerard Johnson. Carved from marble and painted alabaster, it features the two Earls on the same tier, flanking the Countess who is in the centre on a higher tier, the detail and quality of the carving and colouring is stupendous. The Countess' tier is carried on three arches which have typical Elizabethan Renaissance detailing. At the feet and heads of each of the figures are carved heraldic beasts. At each corner of the tomb are very large obelisks. The sides of the tomb reveal carvings of the children, the two girls on the south side being the daughters of the First Earl and the on the north side the Third Earl (of Shakespeare fame) and his sister.

Right next to this monument is a badly damaged, incised Purbeck marble slab, which is the monument to William de Pageham. It is unique, as far as incised monuments in this country are concerned, because its incised lines are in part, left proud of the rest of the slab. This is a French technique, known as Taille d'epargne. The slab depicts a knight under a canopy and dates from around the beginning of the fourteenth century.

Retracing your steps up Church Street,

the view is very photogenic, with the modest Georgian cottages gradually curving round to the church at the bottom. The High Street gives way to the much narrower South Street which almost immediately displays older buildings, with jettied upper stories, half timbering and an altogether different feeling to the rest of the High Street. At right angles to the junction of the High Street and South Street, West Street starts its long upward climb. This street has a varied range of housing, from seventeenth century to modern. Two features of note are to be seen in progressing up the hill. The first of these are three large Sarsen stone boulders, which were uncovered nearby, when the new road to Warsash was being constructed. They were moved to this spot during the 1980s. Higher up the street, set into a bank, is a low fairly nondescript wall, which at first glance merits no further attention. Close examination however reveals that a number of the lower courses of the wall have been built with the knuckle bones of sheep. I am unaware of the employment of such an unusual building material anywhere else in Hampshire. The wall itself is at least two hundred years old. Continue up West Street and Titchfield is shortly left, to be replaced by some fields, larger houses, but most of all by mile after mile of industrial and suburban development.

Warnford

Most people travelling up and down the A32, who bother to stop in Warnford, do so for the George and Falcon. Set on a series of very sharp bends the village is surrounded, perhaps more so than any other, by watercress beds. The clear running water of the River Meon is here diverted through a series of field-sized waterlogged beds of watercress. Surrounding the George and Falcon are a picturesque set of former estate cottages. Stretches of overgrown estate wall, and a surprisingly well kept entrance lodge herald Warnford's and one of Hampshire's loveliest landscaped gardens. Travel further south for some half a mile, and another entrance to the park with public access to the church can be used. The grounds and church have been denuded of the house since its demolition in 1955. This loss merely serves to heighten the quiet beauty of

Warnford – The gatepiers of Warnford Park.

Warnford – Watercress Beds – A Hampshire agricultural speciality.

the park. Many fine trees dot the parkland, running down to the river, which has a small weir and a working miniature water-wheel. The river starts to broaden out, being crossed by a fine bridge with wooden parapets. The view south to the reed edged lake surrounded by trees is outstanding.

When I visited, the presence of humans caused a heron to lazily wheel away over the lake. The picturesque quality of the park is completed by the flock of sheep. Next to the site of the house with its forlorn, isolated fish fountain, is the church of Our Lady. With possibly the finest Norman west tower in the county, the rest of the building is largely Early English. It was built in place of its Saxon predecessor by Adam de Port in approximately 1190. The interior is full of monuments. Outstanding is the seventeenth century one to Sir Thomas Neale, (died 1621), and his two wives. The row of nine children, four of whom carry skulls to show that they died in infancy, is particularly touching. There is a good seventeenth-century screen and tower screen, both date from 1634 and are of archetypal Jacobean style.

To the east of the churchyard are the substantial remains of a mediæval (thirteenth century) aisled hall, with three pillars, one of which rises to almost its full height. This hall, known locally as King John's Hunting Lodge, was undoubtedly of some importance, and deserves, like the adjacent church and landscaped park, to be better known.

West Meon

West Meon – The all pervading presence of the tower of St John the Evangelist.

Another picture postcard village which is situated on a sloping site, bisected by the A32. The village does in fact mark the northernmost point of the Meon Valley before its sharp eastward turn towards East Meon, and the river's source on the flanks of Butser Hill.

The Red Lion with the nearby war memorial set in a triangular parcel of land, is the focal point of the village. Directly up the hill are the Victorian flint built school and schoolhouse which are next to what is one of the largest Victorian churches in Hampshire. The church was rebuilt entirely by G.G.Scott in 1847, one of his earliest large-scale works. With its tall and stately tower,

West Meon – The renewal of a thatched roof.

West Meon – A thatched cottage in need of renewal.

West Meon – A view of the village from the war memorial.

it stamps its presence across the village.

The large surrounding churchyard contains three interesting graves. The first in the older southern graveyard, is a large table tomb to Thomas Lord, after whom a second pub in the village is named. He it was who gave the parcel of land in London which bears his name to this day and is the centre of the cricket world. Fitting indeed that the man is buried in the county which gave the modern game to the world. Its birthplace and cradle is only some four miles distant, at Hambledon. To the north of the church quite near to the tower lies the second burial of note, although far more infamous. On a seemingly nondescript grave cross dedicated to a Mary Burgess is attached a plaque informing us, that this is the final resting place of the ashes of that most notorious of 1960s Russian spies, Guy Burgess. His ashes were brought from Moscow and interred at night in an effort to deter large Press coverage. The third grave is that of the parents of William Cobbett, author of *Rural Rides*. Their grave is not far from that of Thomas Lord, near the wall.

The name Station Road bares testimony to the fact that West Meon once possessed a station on the delightful Meon Valley line. The entire valley still possesses large-scale railway engineering works which have largely been reclaimed by nature.

Wickham – The Old House Hotel and Wickham House, on the north-eastern corner of the square.

Wickham

If you are travelling north up the A32 between Fareham and Alton, you drop imperceptibly into the Meon Valley, which is at this point fairly broad and shallow. On your left-hand side you are soon joined by the overgrown earthworks of the derelict Meon Valley railway line. By the time it is opposite St Nicholas' Church it hides the fact that you are travelling past the village. Turning in under the railway with its iron lattice-work bridge still intact and now a footpath, you find yourself in Bridge Street. The River Meon is almost immediately crossed and north of the bridge is the first building of interest.

Named the Chesapeake Mill it is a large building erected in 1820. But why the strange American name? The answer lies in the fact that the timbers from which the structure of the mill were built were bought from the dockyard at Portsmouth, where the captured American frigate *Chesapeake* was being broken up. The *USS Chesapeake* and the British frigate *HMS Shannon* fought a famous and bloody engagement off Boston in 1813. Nearby is the former village brewery which dates from 1887.

Bridge Street curves and rises towards the as yet unseen square. The houses

Wickham – St Nicholas' Church.

which line Bridge Street are largely of brick although some reveal older façades with half timbering being exposed. As a rule those on the north side are large and impressive, those on the south side far more humble. The most outstanding house in Bridge Street is Queen Lodge a large rambling essay in brick dating from the late seventeenth century. It is of five bays and has a raised central bay with large brick pilasters with Ionic capitals.

The Square comes as a great surprise. A very large space filled on three sides with buildings ranging from half-timbered mediæval buildings to large Georgian houses and later Victorian and twentieth-

Wickham – St Nicholas' Church, the monument to Sir William Uvedale, died 1615.

Left: Wickham – St Nicholas' Church, detail of the monument to Sir William Uvedale, died 1615.

century shops, pubs and houses. Overall however the pervading architectural feeling is that of the Georgian period.

The square and indeed the expansion of Wickham is due to the fact that in 1268 Roger de Secures, the then lord of the manor, was granted the right to hold a market and fair. He would have laid out the large square and this would have started the gradual movement of the village away from the church and manor house which were situated on the eastern bank of the River Meon.

The two most impressive Georgian buildings in the square are the Old House Hotel and Wickham House, which lie in the extreme north-eastern corner. The rest of the eastern side is very modest in scale and possesses most of the shops and the

Wickham – Ivy Cottage, a Victorian flint and brick cottage.

Wickham – The view up Bridge Street, towards the square.

Wickham – Chesapeake Mill, built in 1820.

Wickham – Eastwood House, in the north-western corner of the square.

twentieth-century's contribution. In the south-western corner, what is now Knockers Wine Bar reveals its mid sixteenth-century origins. The rest of the west side is largely Georgian in appearance including The Kings Head pub which purveys good food and a very good pint of Gales Ales. Next to the Kings Head are a pair of two-storey, semi-detached Georgian houses of some architectural pretension. In the north-western corner is Eastwood House. It too has presence created by its large first floor canted bay which is supported on four free-standing piers. No doubt many of the Georgian façades in the square hide mediæval origins.

The northern side is in fact an island infill of modest Georgian and early Victorian buildings. Set back on the bend of Bridge Street, can be seen a flint Victorian cottage, complete with ornate bargeboards and ornate glazing in the windows. The south side of the square was until the late 1960s, simply bounded by the road to Bishops Waltham and a brick garden wall. However H.Hubbard Ford and Associates took on what must surely have been one of the most challenging and difficult pieces of infill imaginable. Their effort although brave, to my mind lacked enough presence to give the south side of the square any sense of presence and architectural merit. The resultant low range of flats already look very dated. A lost opportunity.

The road towards Bishops Waltham has

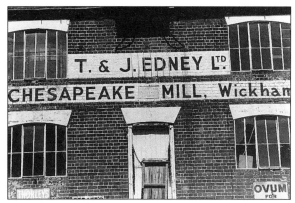

Wickham – Chesapeake Mill, detail of the lettering.

started to be developed with firstly large detached houses and then small estates of executive homes, all very bland and uninspiring. The church at Wickham is, as has already been mentioned, isolated from the rest of the village by both the former railway and the busy A32. St Nicholas' is set upon a large mound which is possibly of prehistoric origins. It was over restored twice in the nineteenth century in 1862 and again between 1872-77. The west tower with its spire is completely Victorian with the exception of the fine Norman doorway which has its original capitals.

There are a few interesting monuments from the old church, two to the Uvedale family, Sir William (died 1615) an elaborate alabaster tomb with the part reclining effigies of him and his wife. This is surrounded by a very large arched canopy with lions, shields and obelisks. On the side of the tomb chest are depicted the nine children, five daughters and four sons, all kneeling. The back of the tomb canopy has a cadaver and a lot of skulls and other emblems of death. There is part of a plain monument to another Uvedale (died 1569).

Until recently the site opposite the church was open fields. Excavations prior to much of the site being developed into a housing estate, revealed the site of a small mediæval building. East from the church, the former rectory is a fine eighteenth-century building. North and east of this is taken up by the Rooksbury Park estate. It was built in 1835 by C.H.Tatham. It is a fine ashlar faced Neo-Classical building with an impressive Ionic columned portic. It now serves as a co-educational preparatory school.

Many have claimed Wickham to be the finest village in the south of England not just Hampshire and a visit to the square, with its fine sense of the scale an the range of buildings which as an ensemble seem to balance, with, in addition the various side streets and the church, surely helps justify this claim. It is fitting that this village should be the birthplace of William of Wykeham, one of the most important figures of the Middle Ages who was born in 1324.

East Hampshire

Hampshire's only true Wealden scenery is to be found in this area. Geologically speaking, this is also the most mixed area in the county. Chalk, Lower Greensand and Upper Greensand and Gault, all meet in this one small area, with the result that the scenery is varied. Steep hills with their scarp faces, more often than not clothed in almost gravity defying, plantations of beech trees, known in Hampshire, as Hangars, the most famous of which is Selborne Hangar. Indeed there is a public footpath which links the various hangars in the area.

There are many fine villages in the area, reflecting the geology and scenery. Chief amongst these is Selborne. Known worldwide for being the home of Gilbert White, the eighteenth-century naturalist, and the setting, for his much loved Natural History, the village does not disappoint. Nearby Chawton, is another international literary mecca, being the one time home of Jane Austen. Hartley Mauditt, is another

classic example of a decayed and deserted village. Just the church, a pond and the odd farm building to keep it company. Colemore, is little more; a gem of a church, surrounded by a small collection of farm buildings and houses. East Tisted and Privett are both outstanding examples of nineteenth-century estate villages.

Chawton

Now thankfully by-passed by the A31 trunk road, it is possible perhaps to capture some of the quiet charm of the village which is known the world over as the place where Jane Austen spent the last eight years of her life. The village is of a straight forward linear pattern, with the church of St Nicholas sited near Chawton House at the southern end of the village. The church was totally rebuilt in 1870 by Sir Arthur Blomfield, and it has a very

impressive tower. Internally a number of features retained from the old church at which Jane Austen had been a regular worshipper. The only items she would perhaps recognise would be the eighteenth-century communion rails and the large marble monument to Sir Richard Price (died 1769). The adjacent Chawton House is of Elizabethan origin with the south front being altered and refaced in the 1630s.

Returning to the village centre past a

Chawton - Thatched cottages on the road to the church.

Chawton - Jane Austen's house.

series of cottages both thatched and tiled, the house on the corner is Jane Austen's house. Now a museum run by Hampshire County Museum Service, it is the mecca for thousands of devotees of Jane Austen's literary works. Rooms are laid out with period furniture and costumes. There are many displays packed with related material. On the opposite side of the road is the almost obligatory tea room and souvenir cum bygones shop. The rest of the street possesses many Georgian and earlier houses and cottages eventually petering out not far short of the A31.

Colemore

Secreted away in a very rural spot of Eastern Hampshire, the hamlet of Colemore is little more than half a dozen cottages and a couple of farms. Adjacent to a series of barns and a farm, is the tiny church of St Peter Ad Vincula. It has been declared redundant since January 1973 and is now cared for by The Redundant Churches Fund. The churchyard, now largely devoid of tombstones often has sheep grazing in it. Thanks to a recent careful restoration (1973-75) the church both internally and externally is in good condition. The rubble walls of the nave and north transept were re-rendered. The chancel and south porch, both of which were rebuilt in 1875 are constructed of flint. The bell cote with its wooden weatherboarding was rebuilt in 1866.

The church was built ambitiously for such a small hamlet, cruciform in plan, although the south transept was demolished in 1670. There is a lovely precise instruction on the door on how to turn the handle. Inside, the church which possesses no electricity, provokes immediately a feeling of age-old simplicity, the smell of candles, the simple furniture. The church in its present form is largely twelfth century, although the north wall of the chancel and the east wall of the north transept both possess windows dating from the eleventh century. There is a twelfth-century square font at the west end of the nave. Nearby hanging from a steel support beam are two bells, one dating from 1380, the other from 1627. The ladder to the former belfry dates from the late seventeenth-century (1694). The pews in the nave date from 1845. The nave is separated by a wooden screen, dating from the fourteenth century, although much rebuilt in 1874. The chancel east window possesses stained glass by C.E.Kempe dating from 1876. In the north transept is a Jacobean altar table. Adjacent to this is a squint and set in the wall an arch with two steps, which are all that remain of the former rood screen.

East Tisted

Anyone driving along the A32 cannot be failed to be impressed by the neat and tidy Victorian estate village which lines the eastern side of the road, as it curves through the well wooded parkland, that forms the greater part of the surrounding countryside. The western side of the valley is composed of Rotherfield Park and the adjoining Pelham Place estate to the north.

Rotherfield Park sits well back in its park, high up on a ridge. It is a mixture of early nineteenth-century Gothic (1851-21), with further mid century Gothic additions in the 1860s and a liberal sprinkling of Elizabethanising later in the century (1890s). The result is a highly romantic lookinghouse, complete with sweeping vistas, magnificent trees and fine gardens. Internally the large hall and staircase is the most impressive of the rooms, all of which possess a well loved family home feeling. The house continues to be home to the Scott family.

From the park, the view back down to the village with its attendant church, the flag of St George flying from the tower, the gently sloping tree filled parkland, is a glorious evocation of the English countryside.

The church of St James was almost totally rebuilt in 1846. It is interesting as a piece of architecture which shows the transition from the archaeologically incorrect Gothic architecture of the early nineteenth century to the more exact styles of the later nineteenth-century High Gothic revivals. One thing that later in the nineteenth century no self-respecting architect would do, would be the use of materials, such as concrete pillars or cast-iron bench ends. The church is particularly well stocked with monuments, many of which come from the earlier church. Three stand out, all to members of the Norton family. They range from Elizabethan Renaissance style to late seventeenth century.

Travelling north from the village, on the right-hand side, again set in splendid parkland scenery, on a small ridge, is Pelham Place. Dating from the early nineteenth century, it is typical of the period with its wide verandahs.

Hartley Mauditt

Yet another classic example of a deserted village site, now marked only by the church and its companion pond. Once there was a thriving hamlet which also possessed a manor house which stood to the south of the church. The manor house was last recorded in the eighteenth century and indeed was demolished before the century was out. The church of St Leonard has therefore stood in splendid isolation for over two hundred years. It consists of a nave with a bell turret at the western end, a south porch, and a chancel, all of which are largely rendered. It smallness means there are no aisles.

Internally the church reveals Norman workmanship, with a very good south doorway, the chancel arch and two small windows. The chancel dates from the thirteenth century and no doubt replaced the Norman apsidal one. There are a series of very good, largely seventeenth-century monuments to the Stuart family. With the sale of the manor by the Stuart family, the house and village entered its final moments. The second Lord Stawell, is supposed to have had the house demolished in 1798 as an act of spite against his wife. Whatever the reason, the demolition of the house would have

Hartley Mauditt – St Leonard's Church and the pond.

Hartley Mauditt – St Leonard's Church and the pond.

hastened the decline of whatever village was left around the church and pond.

Today the scene is incredibly peaceful and very rural, the only company being normally provided by the numerous cows.

Privett

Some five miles north of East Meon, high up on the hill, in very sparsely populated countryside, sits a classic example of a Victorian estate village. It is however an estate village which has been shorn of its house (Basing Park) after only some sixty years of existence. The Nicholson family, who made their fortune through the proceeds from distilling, not only built a large house, but proceeded to endow the village with cottages, a school, and above all else a spectacular and enormous late Victorian church. (This replaced a small church of similar proportion and age to nearby Colemore.) Its tower and spire rises to nearly one hundred and seventy feet above the surrounding countryside. Indeed it acts as a landmark for miles around. The church was designed by Sir Arthur Blomfield and built between 1876 and 1878, at a cost of £22,000 to the Nicholson family. The result is a splendid if somewhat cold and clinical Victorian Gothic church, dedicated to the Holy Trinity.

Externally the building has stone dressings with flint infill. The sense of height and power is further emphasised by the grouping of buttresses and the employment of tall lancet windows. The whole church is designed in the Early English style. Internally the fittings are lavish. The four bay nave rises through a clerestory to a magnificent wooden roof. Most of the windows are filled with stained glass by Heaton Butler and Bayne. The church internally uses a variety of stone and therefore colour, Ham Hill Stone, Bath Stone and Corsehill Stone (honey, cream and red respectively). There is an elaborate stone reredos and Italian marble floors in the sanctuary. Despite having been declared redundant and vested in the Redundant Churches Fund in 1980, and having during the last thirty years, slowly stripped of many of its rich fittings, it still remains a classic example of what late Victorian piety and money could do. The church also possesses a magnificent peal of eight bells (cast in Whitechapel) which on the day I visited, were being rung by a visiting group of campanologists. The large and impressive lych gate is supposed to have been made from timbers from one of the ships of Admiral Parry's expedition to the Arctic. The connection is further strengthened by a series of memorials to members of the Parry family in the church.

Selborne

The very mention of the name Selborne, for many people evokes passages from the work of its most famous son, Gilbert White – visions of an English rural idyll. Yes Selborne is one of the great tourist honeypots of Hampshire and indeed of the South of England.

Drive through it, and the overall impression is of a pretty village hemmed in by both development to the east and west, and the ever present hills.

It is a village which needs to be explored on foot. Apart from the village green in front of the churchyard, the houses seem to turn their back on the road. A series of inviting lanes beckon to be explored. But the best place to start is at the village green. Perhaps the least spoilt part of the village its key feature is now but a sad truncated remnant. The famous yew tree succumbed after well over a thousand years to the gales of 1990. It was replanted under advice but failed to respond.

The church sits in a sloping churchyard. A number of pathways both local and regional pass through it – the adjoining deep valley belongs to the National Trust – they also own the famous Hangar and maintain a car-park. It is worth walking to the other side of this perfect stream filled valley, the view back of the church, churchyard, clusters of roofs against the backdrop of the tree covered hills, is worth the effort. If you continue on this walk, you come to Priory Farm, built near to the site of Selborne Priory, of which not one stone remains visible. It was a foundation of Augustinian Canons and was founded in 1233 by Peter des Roches, the Bishop of Winchester. The priory itself was forced to close in 1484, because of massive debts. There was only one occupant at the end, the prior himself. Extensive excavations have revealed the dimensions and a number of carved stones, tiles and stone coffins, complete

Selborne – St Mary's Church and the sad remnants of the once mighty yew tree.

with skeletons. Much of this is now displayed in the Wakes Museum.

Returning to the church, dedicated to St Mary, with its squat rendered west tower, has much to commend it. Amongst its features are some fine Norman arcades and a Flemish fifteenth-century altarpiece. It was given by Benjamin White as a memorial to his cousin Gilbert White. Typical of the man, he was buried in the churchyard with the simplest of headstones. Not that you are left any

Selborne – Selborne Hangar.

Selborne – The garden front of The Wakes.

detective work to find it, metal signs lead you to it.

Across the green with its almost obligatory art gallery, (although this one is unusual in that it displays the work of disabled artists), lies The Wakes. The home of Gilbert White was this century bought and partially converted into a museum dedicated to the memory of Captain Lawrence Oates of Scott of Antarctic fame. The museum is now splendidly run by the Hampshire Museums Service. Selborne's greatest glory must however be the Wakes gardens and entrancing views of White's beloved Hangar. Hangar is a Hampshire term for one of its most outstanding natural features. The sharp, sometimes almost

sheer scarp (normally northern) faces of the Downs are planted normally with majestic beech plantations. These trees almost defy logic and gravity, seemingly thriving in such conditions.

In the gardens of the Wakes, White constructed a zig-zag path up the side of the hangar. Again an almost obligatory, breathless walk up the side of the hangar to the top reveals a constantly unfolding panorama of Selborne and the surrounding neighbourhood.

A village to explore and savour most certainly, but why oh why have the developers been allowed so much free rein with the infill that has taken place, particularly to the village's eastern approaches?

Southern Hampshire

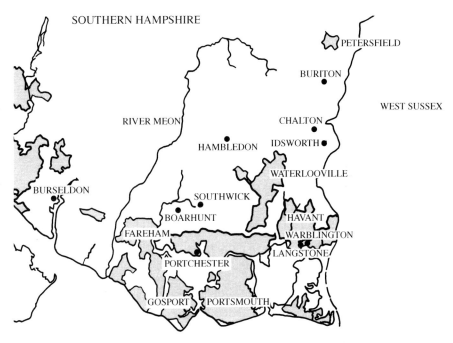

Geologically speaking, this area, is made up almost evenly of Tertiary sands and gravels, which extend along the coastal belt, a thick deposit of London Clay and Chalk, which is mainly in the north and east of the area with the addition of the outlier, comprising Portsdown Hill. This last feature, has helped to shape the urban growth of the region. Southwards, towards the harbour of Portsmouth, is very heavily built up and industrialised. The suburban sprawl of Portsmouth has rapidly filled up neighbouring Gosport and Fareham to the west and Havant, and Emsworth to the east. Northwards over the Portsdown Hill, it is only at the eastern end that suburban spread has flowed up and over and then all the way to the rapidly growing Waterlooville, Denmead, Cowplain, Catherington, Lovedean and Horndean.

Outside of this suburban spread, the countryside and the villages are relatively unspoilt. Indeed the physical presence of Portsdown Hill has, with the exception of the eastern end, managed to act as a full stop to the growth of suburbia. Yet amongst all this development on the coastal fringe are some remarkable survivals. At the top end of the almost totally undeveloped Langstone Harbour are the near neighbours of Langstone and Warblington. Even more miraculous a survival is the original village and castle of Portchester, at the top end of Portsmouth Harbour. Portchester, is the finest surviving castle in Hampshire and has some of the best Roman walls, north of the alps. One further nautical flavoured village, is Burseldon on the Hamble River. Inland and at the foot of Portsdown Hill's northern face, is Southwick, redolent with history, it was from here that D-Day was launched. Set into a fold of the northern flank of Portsdown Hill, is tiny Boarhunt. Northwards and on to the chalk, is Hambledon, famous the world over as the birthplace of the game of cricket. Eastwards and running down the border with West Sussex are the villages of Buriton, which sits on the edge, geologically speaking, between Chalk and Upper Greensand and Gault, and in folds of the Chalk South Downs, Chalton and Idsworth, the last named, another deserted settlement, where just the church sits on a knoll, with a handful of cottages and a couple of larger houses scattered around.

Boarhunt

It is amazing what the massive bulk of Portsdown Hill rising some five hundred feet has done for this particular patch of south Hampshire. Without it the villages of Southwick and the Boarhunts along with many square miles of prime agricultural land and woods, would have been engulfed in a northward tidal wave of suburban expansion from Portsmouth. To stand on Portsdown Hill is therefore somewhat of a schizophrenic event. To the south proudly stretches Portsmouth (the

Boarhunt – St Nicholas' Church.

only city in Britain to be built on an island) and its magnificent harbour, its suburbs, the Solent and the view of the Isle of Wight. To the west Southampton Water, the sprawl of Southampton, the industrial complexes of Fawley and Calshot, with the New Forest behind them. To the east Langstone Harbour, Hayling Island, Chichester Harbour and in the distance Chichester Cathedral, Bognor Regis and Selsey Bill. Turn northwards and the view is apparently one of continuous open rolling countryside, a patchwork of fields, woods, with on the horizon the majestic bulk of the Hampshire Downs, culminating in Butser Hill. Further to the east the Sussex Downs with Stoughton Down and the Trundle appear prominent. Only to the east around Waterlooville is the view at all urbanised in appearance.

In the immediate foreground, large fields of corn roll down towards the cluster of roofs that is Southwick. Set in a fold at the western end of Portsdown Hill is Boarhunt. This is not a village merely a single cottage, a farm and a wonderful survival from the very eve of the Norman conquest, St Nicholas' Church. It is a simple two cell building which has been ascribed the date of *c.*1064. It has only the addition of a small Victorian bell turret at the west end and the replacement of most of the double splayed Saxon windows, by thirteenth-century lancets and, a later Tudor window to alter its Saxon lines. Internally the 1853 restoration added the pitch pine furnishings, box pews, a three-decker pulpit, communion rails, west gallery. All incredibly out of date and step for that date and thank goodness for that.

The village if it can be called that, of North Boarhunt is about a mile and a half to the north. A simple straggle of mainly brick cottages and small holdings (there is also a garage) that stretch on either side of the road from Southwick to Wickham.

Buriton

A scenically stunning village, which nestles at the foot of the steep north scarp of the chalk downs, which having so recently left the massive bulk of Butser Hill, are now striding along towards the nearby Sussex border and Harting Down. Geologically speaking the village sits on the very boundary between chalk and greensand. Hence the preponderance of sunken lanes and indeed the employment of the local malmstone. The village itself surrounds a well kept and reasonably large pond, overhung by trees. Adjacent to this on the eastern side is the church and the adjoining manor house.

The church of St Mary has a west tower, rebuilt in 1714. It is however the interior which calls for attention with four bays separated by large round twelfth-century piers and scalloped capitals. Outside a walk through the churchyard opens up some of the most magnificent views, in Hampshire, of the thickly wooded, steep slopes of the downs.

The manor house was the boyhood home of Edward Gibbon who wrote *The Decline and Fall of the Roman Empire.*

Buriton – The Manor House.

Buriton – The village pond.

Buriton – St Mary's Church.

The house itself is partially hidden by outbuildings (which have been converted into very desirable residences themselves) and the church. It consists of a typical brick, small Georgian house of no great architectural pretensions. This house and its gardens along with half a dozen other houses and their gardens, a number of which border the pond, are open once a year. It is a good way to see the village and its secrets. There is for instance a garden with a large lake much higher up almost against the embankment of the main London to Portsmouth railway line, as it makes its final approach to Buriton tunnel. Indeed the clatter of the trains and the sounding of their horns as they plunge into the tunnel, make an audible rather than visible intrusion into the rustic charms of the village.

Burseldon

A village with many faces. Its famous waterside pub, The Jolly Sailor, became known to millions through the television soap opera *Howards Way*. At any time of the year it is the Hamble River and the multitude of boats which is the sole reason for thousands of people to pour in. Indeed it often seems from the steep almost cliff

Burseldon – View down a village street.

Burseldon – Moorings on the Hamble.

Burseldon − The waterside.

like bluffs that you could almost cross the river by walking on boats. It is also an enormous display of wealth. Since the middle ages the area has been noted for shipbuilding and today is no exception, with the old A27 being lined by shipyards and builders, such as Moody's. The railway line from Portsmouth to South-ampton, having been brought in across the river on a box girder bridge on massive piers, is served by a nondescript and modern railway station. It does however have a centrally placed car park, which is the best place to start an exploration on foot. (The railway line at this point plunges into a deep cutting as it heads towards Southampton.)

Much of the original village fills the steep slopes up from the river, a mixture of Georgian houses, Victorian cottages and a lot of more recent suburban infill. At the top of the hill are some very large houses, behind high walls and hedges. This pattern is continued down the long dead end road that follows the river bank. There is no real centre to the village and it straggles across a large area. There is a Roman Catholic Chapel of Our Lady of the Rosary, which appears to be part of a large house. Of no merit architecturally, (it was built in 1906), it, as with most things in this village, suddenly looms up without warning. The church of St Leonard, is set in a wooded situation with no real connection to the various parts of Burseldon already discussed, or indeed the vast suburban estates which have gradually encroached from the Southampton direction. It is largely the product of a wholesale 1888 remodelling by John Dando Sedding. He kept some of the thirteenth-century features, but not much.

Back out on the main road, at the top of the hill is the now restored windmill, which was first built in 1814. Of Burseldon's other former large-scale industry, brickmaking, little now remains.

Chalton

A very dramatically situated village, high up in a fold of the South Downs, not far from the mighty bulk of Butser Hill. The village is 'signposted' for some considerable distance, by the recently restored (1980) windmill. If you travel in along the narrow lanes from the west and the A3, you also pass the reconstructed Iron Age farmstead, which, with its large circular thatched hut and various pits nestling in the bottom of a fold of Windmill Hill, is in itself well worth a visit. Nearby on Church Down, behind the church, extensive excavations undertaken by Professor Barry Cunliffe and a team of archaeologists, from Southampton University, in the early 1970s, uncovered the extensive post-hole remains of a large Saxon rectangular building. Gradually, the settlement patterns changed, and the village settled further down the hill around the present church and sloping green. The resultant village is exceptionally pretty. The central feature being the famous thatched, white painted, half-timbered, Red Lion pub, with its large Inglenook fireplace. This building has in recent years received sympathetic exten-sions to the rear. Across the road, the triangular green, complete with pub sign, slopes up steeply to a number of cottages

Chalton – The Red Lion.

Chalton – St Michael's Church.

and the gate to the church. The church is dedicated to St Michael and is for the size of the village impressive. The whole fabric is built of flint with stone dressing, and dates mainly from the thirteenth century. The Chancel is particularly splendid with, at the sides, good tall, slender lancet windows. The east end has a magnificent four light lancet window, with three quatrefoil lights above. Such are the ample proportions of the nave, south chapel and chancel, that the tower appears from the east to be rather small and insignificant. The view from the top corner of the churchyard of the church, is particularly memorable.

Internally, there is a small but good Jacobean monument to Richard Ball, a rector who died in 1632. It depicts a small kneeling figure in clerical robes, set under an entablature carried on Corinthian columns.

Adjacent to the church on the left-hand side, is a building known as the Priory. Although there is evidence that the building has mediæval and Tudor antecedants, the present building, which was formerly the Rectory, has a front which dates apparently from the mid eighteenth century, and is of flint construction with red brick dressings. To the north the village contains a small number of estate cottages, dating from the nineteenth century.

Hambledon – St Peter and St Paul's Church.

Hambledon

A name synonymous with cricket, the village is famed worldwide as the birthplace of the game. This took place on Broadhalfpenny Down, just to the north of the village. A cricket pitch is still there along with an impressive memorial to the fact. This is opposite the Bat and Ball Inn which has recently suffered the ignominy of having its name adulterated. It now has the addition of the name Natterjacks. This building itself is pleasing, being largely tile hung and whitewashed.

Returning to the village, which stretches along the bottom of a steep sided, and narrow chalk valley. A good place to start any walk is at the foot of the churchyard. The view either up or down this street, with the church at the top, is often reproduced in paintings and photographs. It is lined largely with Georgian houses. The houses at right angles at the bottom not only are whitewashed, with twentieth-century shop façades, but completely mar the view, with the very large letters informing us that the building is a 'Peoples Market'. Where were the planners when this was allowed? Behind this, rises up the wooded southern slope dotted with

Hambledon – The village houses sloping down the valley sides.

houses. The main street in each direction possesses the usual Hampshire village mix of houses of varying size, date and construction, although the undeniable feel is of the Georgian period. Towards the northern edge of the village, the houses thin out and are interspersed with altogether larger and more impressive individual dwellings.

The church of St Peter and St Paul is a very large and complex building with evidence of every architectural style from the Saxon period onwards. Externally the large churchyard setting and indeed the hillside situation can be best appreciated by walking to the top, extreme north-western corner of the churchyard. This reveals the length and size of the church. As with so many, the village church is

Hambledon – Commemoration stone, on Broadhalfpenny Down, to the birthplace of cricket.

constructed with the most common local material – flint for the infill.

It comprises a west tower which was rebuilt after a fire in 1794, a two-storey vestry attached to the tower, a two-storey porch, a long nave, aisles and a long chancel. Internally the evidence of a more or less continuous process of enlargement is obvious. Saxon work which was once external, is exposed in the upper part of the nave arcading. There are Norman pillars and windows. The original chancel arch dating from the thirteenth century was left *in situ*, when the nave was extended. What was the original chancel, became an eastward extension of the nave, and a new chancel was added. Most of the roofs in the church are the original mediæval ones. The church was reasonably restored by Ewan Christian in 1876. There are a range of mainly eighteenth-century monuments and a large amount of Victorian stained glass. When you have wandered around the churchyard, look to the eastern edge and amongst the trees, in a garden is a folly, which is an imitation church tower, built of brick.

Idsworth

Right on the border between Hampshire and West Sussex, in a remote fold of the chalk downs lies one of Hampshire's most prized architectural treasures. It cannot be classed as a hamlet and certainly not a village. What it is, is a small church on a knoll in the middle of a field, with nearby the converted former stables, and walled garden of the long demolished manor house. Nearby are a number of cottages and a farm. This idyllic rural scene is punctured on average, about every twenty minutes during the week, as the main London – Portsmouth railway line runs along the bottom of the valley. Next to this runs the small lane which links Idsworth with neighbouring Finchdean and Rowlands Castle. It was the coming of the railway which caused the owner of the manor to demolish the house, and build a new mansion in the latest Neo-Jacobean style, over the ridge of the valley to the west. All that remains now besides the stables, are an imposing avenue of trees marching down the side of the valley to meet the railway line.

Turning to St Hubert's Church, it is a simple nave, and chancel with a wooden boarded bell tower at the eastern end of the nave. It is constructed with flint infill and from the outside appears as a perfect example of a small mediæval church. Internally this feeling of a church untouched by the Victorians seems complete. For most of the nineteenth century it was derelict, and from 1912-14 it was very carefully restored by H.S.Goodhart-Rendel. He it was who was responsible for making such a good job, that it is difficult for all but the most experienced eye, to tell apart the twentieth century from the eighteenth. A west gallery, box pews and a real Jacobean pulpit all add to the quality of rustic simplicity. It is however in the chancel that the church's claim to fame, on a regional even national level resides. For large parts of the north wall, and to a

Idsworth – St Hubert's Church, alone in the fields.

lesser extent the east and south walls, possess a series of paintings dating from the early 1300s. They are with the exception of the wall paintings in Winchester Cathedral the most important in Hampshire. They represent in two tiers, hunting scenes connected with the life of St Hubert, and scenes from the story of St John the Baptist. There are also figures of St Peter, St Paul and various angels.

At any stage of the year, this quiet spot exerts its calming influence, but for me two times stand out as memorable to visit. The hardness of winter, with the ploughed fields and bare trees on the background hills, and in complete contrast early summer, especially if the surrounding field is planted with a crop of oil seed rape, when the little church seems to be floating on a yellow sea.

Langstone

This is one of those rare commodities along Hampshire's seaboard – a village where the sense of bonding with the sea – its sight and smell are integral to its charms. Unlike Bucklers Hard this village is unprepossessing. It's not a tourist honeypot, there are no museums. Even its

location, the traditional bridgehead to Hayling Island, hemmed in to the north by the industrial and suburban sprawl of Havant, just seems to underline its miraculous survival.

At first glance a long street full of character vernacular houses, from a range

Langstone – The tide and wind mills.

Langstone – The Royal Oak and neighbouring mills.

of periods and styles, humble rather than imposing. The end of the street beckons you with a view of the sea, boats and Hayling Island. At the seaward end you are greeted by one of, to my mind, the most memorable visions of the south coast. It is a combination of pub (The Royal Oak), houses, tide mill and black painted windmill with the receding tree-lined coast with the ruins of Warblington Castle and its attendant church in the middle distance, and the South Downs as a backdrop.

This scene alters with every changing nuance of lighting and tide conditions. Fortunately the coastal path allows this group of buildings to be seen from a number of directions. The tide mill and windmill are a rare combination and a rarer survival, which have been and remain the inspiration for numerous paintings by local artists.

Portchester

The most complete and impressive Roman walls north of the Alps, enclose in one corner a royal Norman castle, and in the opposite corner a Norman priory church. These are the bare facts of what is Hampshire's most impressive castle. Its

Portchester – The Roman walls of the castle.

situation, on a low spur of land jutting out into the northern edge of Portsmouth Harbour, surrounded on all sides by suburbia, industrial complexes and all the other paraphanelia of a large twentieth-century city, merely serves to highlight the almost miraculous survival. Seen from a distance, because of its low lying situation, the castle appears non too impressive. From on top of nearby Portsdown Hill it is overshadowed by the neighbouring shipbuilders, and one's view is always drawn to the adjacent harbour and the vast panoramic view of the city of Portsmouth, the naval base, ships of all description, the sea and the Isle of Wight. From the M275 motorway bridge and embankment it appears far more impressive.

The castle was the reason for Portchester's existence and the slight remains of Bronze age earthworks reveal a long tradition of using this easily defendable neck of land. Before returning to discuss the castle and church, what of the rest of the village? Its present size is the result of massive suburban expansion between the two World Wars, by Portsmouth. Housing estates expanded up the slopes of Portsdown Hill and along the edge of both the harbour and Fareham Creek.

There was an earlier expansion away from the castle, during the Victorian period, around the old A27 and the new

Portchester – The Norman castle in the north-western corner of the Roman fort.

railway line. Most of this area, known as 'the crossroads' has been over the last twenty-five years ruthlessly swept away. Such buildings as the bakery, a pub, a convent, a confectioners, blacksmith's, a chalk by-products factory, large residential houses, have all made way for road expansion and new shop and industrial units. However, travel some half a mile south down Castle Street, and as the street gently curves, the houses become older. Thatched brick cottages, mingle with more substantial Georgian houses and weather-boarded houses. Mature trees and gardens appear, as the road broadens out into almost a square, containing a small green with an oak tree. Set around this are again a range of vernacular styles and periods,

with some very impressive houses interspersed. On the south-eastern side, the houses stop and quite suddenly you are confronted with a view through the trees, of the sheer hundred-foot plus smooth ashlar faced stone wall of the Norman keep. Another glance reveals the rubble and flint core of the Roman walls punctuated by the Roman bastions. To either side are glimpses of the sea.

The castle (now in the protection of English Heritage) was begun by the Romans in the latter stages of the third century AD (it was the most westerly of the Saxon Shore Forts). Covering some eight acres it was a rectangular enclosure defended by stone walls some twenty feet high and ten feet thick. There were also

Portchester – Eighteenth and nineteenth-century houses.

twenty semi-circular bastions of which fourteen survive, and can be most readily appreciated along the southern wall. That these walls survive to their full height, and although halved in thickness, were strong enough to be used as part of the mediæval fortifications, is testament to the quality of Roman workmanship. The two main Roman gateways have been replaced by more elaborate mediæval gateways. In the north-west angle of the Roman fort, the Normans proceeded to erect (*c.*1120) a castle, with the immense keep built into the Roman wall (which survives to full thickness at this point). They dug a small moat, complete with drawbridge and inner walls. This small inner ward was later turned into a palace by Richard II, and although a roofless shell, enough remains to appreciate the high quality of the workmanship. The keep today houses a highly imaginative display on the development of the site and the related historical events, and for those who do not suffer from vertigo, the view from the top is tremendous. The castle became the chief embarkation point for many of the invasions and wars with France. Indeed it was from here that Henry V and his army assembled before setting out on the

Portchester – Eighteenth-century houses in Castle Street.

campaign which finished with Agincourt. Across the harbour the expansion of Portsmouth into the premier naval base of Britain, spelt a long slow decay for Portchester Castle. As a result it was spared significant damage in the Civil War. It briefly came into its own again during the eighteenth and nineteenth century wars with France when it became a vast prisoner of war camp. In the south-eastern corner of the fort is the Norman priory church of St Mary's. It was started in 1145, and the church complete with its cloister and conventual buildings nestled behind the walls of the fort, was in existence for barely a decade before the monks moved over the hill to a new location at Southwick. (Southwick Priory would prosper to such an extent, to become regionally important both in terms of economic prosperity and indeed its cultural and artistic legacy.) So today the church is shorn of its south transepts and all the other related conventual buildings. In the Roman wall are the remains of arcading over the latrines, which pierced the wall at this point. Externally the church sits low and squat, a central tower which barely breaks the pitch line of the nave roof and a west end which possesses two very large clasping buttresses. The west door is very ornate with three bands of decoration. Above the door is an arcade of three round headed arches, the middle one being glazed. There is little in the way of external decorative features and the severe appearance is continued inside. Over the site of part of the cloisters in 1977, a new parish room was constructed. Modern and low it sits very incongruous in such a historic setting.

The church interior suffered a particularly severe scrape during the restoration of 1888-89, which only emphasises the austere nature of the building. Just by the west door is the very ornate mid twelfth-century font (on a nineteenth-century base). The decoration consists of intersecting arches, highly decorated with depictions of all manner of birds, beasts and humans. This could possibly be a depiction of the Garden of Eden. There is a large hatchment on the wall dating from 1705 and commemorating the generosity of Queen Anne in giving timber and money towards the repair of the church. (The church incidentally was reopened in 1710.) There

are a number of monuments in the church, the most notable being that to Sir Thomas Cornwallis (died 1618) who was both Governor of the castle and Groom Porter to Queen Elizabeth I. He had been responsible for the rebuilding of the chancel, the closing off of the south transept, and general repairs to the church which had by all accounts become virtually ruinous. His bust, was made by one of the most important stone carvers of the day, Nicholas Stone. Amongst the many tombs and memorials in the graveyard is that to William Wyllie, the famous marine artist.

A walk, outside, around the circuit of walls, is essential and reveals a constantly changing series of views. To the north and close by is the active Vosper's shipyard. Frequently there is a fast patrol craft, nearing completion on the slipway. Behind this rises the bulk of Portsdown Hill. Eastwards and now very close is the reclaimed land that has become Port Solent Marina. Southwards is the view down the harbour to the tower blocks, spires, masts, cranes etc of Portsmouth. Closer to are the lines of mothballed navy ships silently awaiting their fate.

Southwick

Nestling at the foot of the northern slopes of Portsdown, the village has mercifully been given a by-pass which now means that it is an act of deliberation to enter the village. Coming up the low rise from the modern roundabout you are immediately met by signs welcoming you to the D-Day village, followed shortly after by a set of allied nation flags. The road to *HMS*

Dryad, the Admiralty shore establishment, which was the centre for the planning and initial implementation of the Allies invasion of France, forks off to the right. The village street continues with the first of its two pubs on the right-hand side. A plaque records that Generals Montgomery and Eisenhower drank in here and, what they had (such it seems is the public

Southwick – View of the church of St James. Without the Priory and adjoining houses.

appetite for the trivial, some fifty years on). What strikes you immediately is the uniformity of the paintwork of the village, a strikingly rich maroon/red. For Southwick is an estate village par excellence. It was until 1988 owned by the Borthwick-Norton family. However in that year Mrs Eva Borthwick Norton, then in her nineties, died and left her entire estate to her nephew Mr R.Thistlethwaite, along with two important paintings to a museum in Edinburgh.

This was a newsworthy event which thrust Southwick briefly into the national limelight for a moment. The estate still owns virtually everything in the parish, and the most obvious manifestation of this is the uniformity in colour of paintwork.

The village has not one style of architecture but many examples of a whole range of vernacular styles, from small timber-framed cottages, a rare weatherboarded and thatched cottage, through larger brick houses, to a handful of imposing stone faced houses, especially in West Street.

Just up the hill from the Golden Lion pub and adjacent to the churchyard wall is a small patch of green complete with a pump. This acts as a foil to a row of four cottages, half timbered at each end and brick Georgian faced cottages in the middle. The middle cottage also possesses a Georgian doorcase. Opposite these are a range of buildings including the village post office. The church behind its high

Southwick – Thatched cottage in West Street.

Southwick – The view up West Street towards the church.

wall seemingly juts out into the street. Its west tower acts a pivotal focal point whether you are driving or walking from north, south or west. Its name St James Without the Priory Gate is the first hint that Southwick owes its existence to the move, sometime between 1145-53, by Augustinian Canons from the military environment of Portchester Castle, just over Portsdown Hill. The priory itself rose to regional eminence, monks from here setting up what was to become Portsmouth Cathedral. It is also open to some debate as to whether it was from here that the craftsmen who designed and built the Transitional arcades of Portsmouth Cathedral and possibly built or if not influenced Boxgrove Priory and

Chichester Cathedral, were based. The site was quickly demolished at the Dissolution in 1538 and replaced by a series of ever bigger mansions and landscaped grounds. To this I will return. The priory site itself although never fully excavated, has in recent years been the subject of a series of systematic investigations. It is now believed that the church was in size equal to that of Chichester Cathedral.

The church itself although dating from the Norman period was almost totally rebuilt in 1566 by John Whyte, who had purchased the monastery site at the Dissolution. As a result a number of windows and capitals of very fine workmanship, found their way into the fabric of the church. He himself is buried

Southwick – Weatherboarded cottage in West Street.

in an impressive tomb chest set into the north wall of the chancel, which has in effect, formed an arch which is supported by Doric columns, which themselves are surmounted by small pediments, which in turn flank a larger central pediment which has inset the arms of John Whyte. On the apex of each pediment is a cherub holding a shield. The actual tomb chest has on its sides, decoration made up of quatrefoil patterns and on top the brasses set in to him, his wife and children. The east end of the church is taken up by a large eighteenth-century reredos, which is classical in its inspiration, also blocks much of the east window. The communion rails are eighteenth century and are reminiscent of the large wooden pillars at the west end which support the gallery. There are a small number of family pews surviving, which give an indication of how homely the church must have formerly felt. One further note of interest is that the church is known as a Peculiar, which means that the church is exempt from Diocesan jurisdiction. The owner of the estate holds the following titles, Lay Prior, Ordinary, Patron and Rector of the Peculiar and Parish of Southwick.

Opposite the church is the former Victorian school constructed out of knapped flint. It is now a series of offices. West Street has a whole range of buildings which on the southern side sit on top of well kept grassy banks. Halfway down on the northern side is the imposing early nineteenth-century estate office. Running north from the church another street has a terrace of cottages on a raised bank and the second pub, The Red Lion. Beyond this the village gradually peters out.

There is an adjoining almost separate village behind the church to the east. This is the married quarters of *HMS Dryad*. *HMS Dryad* was moved out of Portsmouth Dockyard during the war to what was then the Mansion and grounds to which the village was attached. It has remained in Admiralty hands ever since. It was this reason that just prior to D-Day it became the headquarters for General Eisenhower and the Chiefs of Staff. Today the operations room with its map of the Normandy landing sites, is frozen in time, a memorial to a moment when this one tiny Hampshire village played host to one of the most momentous moments in twentieth-century history. The house itself is the latest in a line of mansions which have adorned the location since the Dissolution of the priory in 1538. At one stage there were superb formal grounds and terraces which were in turn swept away as fashion

Southwick – Georgian doorcase in estate regulation maroon.

dictated by more naturalistic landscaping. Today as you drive down the side of Portsdown Hill you can see the house surrounded by modern low rise office and accommodation blocks. In the foreground acting as a foil to the golf course which has been created is a stretch of walling with a mediæval gate which is all that is visible from the former magnificent priory.

Warblington

Isolated from the suburban tentacles of both Emsworth and Havant, by a combination of dual carriageways and the precious survival of farmland, Warblington, which was once the mother parish for Emsworth, is today just a cluster of farm buildings, the ruins of the castle and its adjoining farmhouse, the church and the related extensive graveyards. All this is set against the backdrop of the sea and the rural outline of Hayling Island. Warb-

lington's most prominent feature the castle, was never in fact a castle, but rather a very large and sumptuous Tudor fortified mansion, that was the principal residence of Margaret Pole, Countess of Salisbury. She was the last of the Plantagenets in the House of York and as such was walking a political tightrope that would eventually, through no fault of her own, cost her, her life. Such was her importance that she was visited by the King at Warblington in

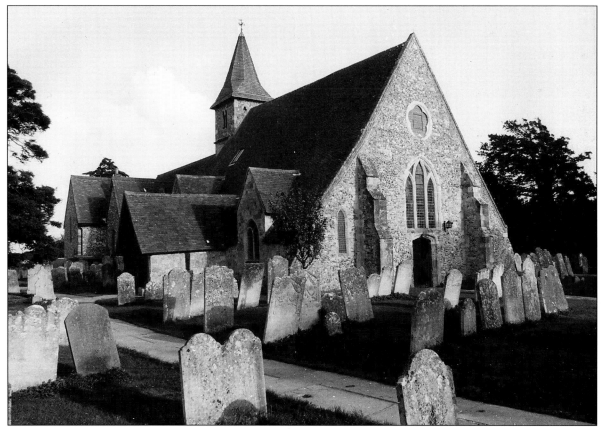

Warblington – The church of St Thomas à Becket.

1526. She even at one stage became Governess to Princess Mary. Between 1515 and 1525 a large up-to-date mansion was erected. Henry VIII in a fit of conscience, saw fit to return some of the titles and estates his father had appropriated and, as a result of being given back some of her family's confiscated estates, she chose the site at Warblington, which was by this time if not completely deserted, then most certainly well on the way.

There had been a previous manor house, although not on any scale. In fact Warblington has been inhabited since the Roman period. (The evidence of extensive Roman buildings, possibly a villa, have been located in the adjacent fields to the east of the church.) The house she proceeded to build was in plan a square courtyard building surrounded by a moat. The gateway was an impressive affair, with four octagonal turrets rising above the rest of the fabric of the house. Some idea of the appearance of the house can be gleaned from the ruins of Titchfield Abbey. The house was described in some detail just prior to the Civil War in the 1630s, 'a very fair place, well moated about, built all of bricks and stones, and is of great receipt, built square in length two hundred feet, and in breadth two hundred feet, with a fair green court within, and the buildings around the said court, with a fair gallery and divers chambers of great count, and four towers covered with lead,

Warblington – The shattered fragment of Warblington Castle.

and a very great and spacious hall, parlour and great chamber, and all other houses or offices whatsoever necessary for such a house and a very fair chapel within the said house, and the place all covered with tiles and stones...' The hall was some fifty-eight feet long by thirty-two feet wide.

The Civil War was Warblington's nemesis. It was held by the Cotton family for the King and was first seized by Parliament in 1643. In the same year it was retaken by the Royalists after a long siege. In the summer of 1644 the Royalists abandoned it and retreated. Upon seizing it for a second time, the Parliamentarians 'slighted' the castle. Today a few meagre walls, the outer arch and one of the four crenellated octagonal turrets bare witness

to a tumultuous period in our history. The present farmhouse built on the site, dates from the late seventeenth century. This is surrounded by farm buildings of mostly modern construction, although there is a large weatherboard barn. It is an active dairy and dairy farm and the smell is often pungent.

The church is surprisingly large, with steeply pitched roofs sloping almost to the ground covering nave and aisles in one single large surface, which is punctuated by dormer windows. The central tower is very small, being almost overwhelmed by the large nave. It has three stages, the top one only just clearing the apex of the nave and is surmounted by a small spire. The bottom stage reveals the Saxon origins of the church with a perfectly-preserved arch dating from this period. There is one on either visible face of the tower. This stage of the tower also has Roman bricks and tiles incorporated. No doubt the adjacent Roman ruins were a good local quarry. Most of the church was built in the late twelfth and early thirteenth century, with two small scale restorations in the nineteenth century. The chancel which unusually is longer than the nave, is thought to be built over the site of the Saxon church. Both aisles contain good fourteenth-century tombs of women. The north porch has a good example of fourteenth-century woodwork.

The churchyard is one of the best that I know, full of interesting gravestones of some artistic merit. Those from the eighteenth century possess some fine carving depicting the incidents which caused the deaths of those being remembered. There is a masted ship upside down amongst the waves in Dublin Harbour. Another of the masted ship *HMS Torbay* on fire in Portsmouth Harbour. Cartouches, skulls and angels abound and half an hour spent wandering around the churchyard is well repaid. Near the north porch is the grave of the first Bishop of Adelaide (Australia).

In the north-west and south-east corners of the churchyard are two, possibly unique buildings. They are single-storey flint built, square huts, which were erected early in the nineteenth century, as nightwatchmen's huts. They were employ-

Warblington – One of a pair of early nineteenth-century watchmen's huts, built to protect the cemetery and stop grave robbing.

ed to stop recently buried bodies being exhumed and taken away and sold to be used for medical purposes. There are also a number of yew trees in the churchyard including a magnificent specimen, with a girth of some twenty-six feet. It was growing at least as long ago as the foundation of the Saxon church.

Bibliography

Hidden Hampshire, John Barton, Countryside Books 1989. Reprinted 1991.

Hampshire the Complete Guide, Jo Draper, Dovecote Press Ltd 1990.

Hampshire Curiosities: A Guide to Follies, Curious Tales, Unusual People & Architectural Eccentricities, Jo Draper, Dovecote Press 1989.

A Hampshire Manor:- Hinton Ampner, Ralph Dutton, First published in 1968 by BT Batsford. This edition published in 1988 by Century in association with The National Trust.

Hampshire, Ralph Dutton, BT Batsford 1970.
Exploring Villages, Joscelyne Finberg, Routledge & Kegan Paul 1958.

Wessex Has Their Bones, Douglas Greenwood, Roy Gasson Associates 1985.

English landscapes, WG Hoskins, Published by the BBC 1973, Reprinted 1974, 1976 (three times) 1979, 1980.

Blue Guide Churches and Chapels Southern England, Edited by Stephen C.Humphrey, *Hampshire* by Michael Hope, A & C Black 1991.

The Face of Britain:- English Downland, H.J.Massingham, Published by BT Batsford 1936, 1942, 1949.

The Kings England – Hampshire with the Isle of Wight, Arthur Mee (revised by ET Long), First published in 1939, Sixth impression 1956.

This edition Hodder and Stoughton 1967.
The Buildings of England:- Hampshire and The Isle of Wight, Nikolaus Pevsner and David Lloyd, Penguin Books Ltd. First published 1967 and reprinted 1973, 1979.

The Common Lands of Hampshire, L.E.Taverner, Hampshire County Council 1957.

Hampshire and the Isle of Wight, Brian Vesey-Fitzgerald, Robert Hale Ltd 1949.

Structure Surface and Drainage in South East England, S.W.Wooldridge and D.L.Linton, George Philip and Son Ltd. First published 1955, Second Impression 1964.

The New Hampshire Village Book, Hampshire Federation of Women's Institutes, Hampshire Federation of Women's Institutes and Countryside Books 1990.

In addition there are the numerous individual village and church pamphlets, guides to indivdual sites such as Portchester Castle.

The county is singularly blessed in having the long-established monthly magazine *Hampshire the County,* published by Paul Cave publications.

Index